# Teach Your Herding Breed to be a Great Companion Dog

## From Obsessive to Outstanding

Dawn Antoniak-Mitchell, Esq., MPA, CPDT-KSA, CBCC-KA

Dogwise Publishing

Wenatchee, Washington U.S.A.

**Teach Your Herding Breed to be a Great Companion Dog**
**From Obsessive to Outstanding**
Dawn Antoniak-Mitchell, Esq., MPA, CPDT-KSA, CBCC-KA

Dogwise Publishing
A Division of Direct Book Service, Inc.
403 South Mission Street, Wenatchee, Washington 98801
1-509-663-9115, 1-800-776-2665
www.dogwisepublishing.com / info@dogwisepublishing.com

Editor in chief: Larry Woodward
Photos: Dawn Antoniak-Mitchell, Jeff Bream, Patty Mlsna Curry, Gloria Hartshorn, Robert San-
ford, Dianne Krantz, Cindy Mendonca, Jeff Mitchell, Melissa Myers, National Media Library un-
der common use license, Carole Sewell, Ami Sheffield, Nate Standish, and Marabeth White.
Graphic design: Lindsay Peternell
Cover design: Jesus Cordero

Library of Congress Cataloging-in-Publication Data
Antoniak-Mitchell, Dawn, 1966-
  Teach your herding breed to be a great companion dog : from obsessive to outstanding /
Dawn Antoniak-Mitchell, Esq., MPA, CPDT-KSA, CBCC-KA.
     pages cm
  Includes index.
  ISBN 978-1-61781-162-3
  1. Herding dogs--Training. 2. Herding dogs--Behavior. I. Title.
  SF428.6.A58 2015
  636.737--dc23
                        2015015059

ISBN: 978-1617811-62-3

Printed in the U.S.A.

*To Gabriel,*

*who taught me to gather all*
*good things in life together*

# Contents

# Acknowledgments

For the third time, I would like to start by thanking everyone at Dogwise for giving me the opportunity to bring another training book to completion. Your continued support is truly appreciated.

Thank you to Jeff for his patience with yet another book project. You are the only person who actually understands the method to my madness when I write. And the futility of arguing with it.

Thank you to all my BonaFide Dog Academy students and fellow dog trainers the world over who graciously helped me obtain photographs. Pictures speak far more than a thousand words when those images capture the intelligence, spirit, and determination of herding dogs. And a huge shout-out to Robert Sanford, a cat person at heart, who capably translated my cryptic dog-training instructions into lovely photographs.

The past informs the present, and, as a result, no one ever develops a completely novel approach to dog training. Many of the exercises and games in this book are adaptations of ideas from well-known researchers and trainers such as Jean Donaldson, Karen Pryor, Patricia McConnell, Brenda Aloff, Kay Laurence, Turid Rugaas, and Sylvia Bishop, as well as lesser-known, but equally talented, trainers and herding dog fanciers of the past and present. Thank you for laying the foundation for future generations of trainers to build upon.

The biggest debt of gratitude I owe is to the generations of herding dog owners everywhere who created, adapted, protected, worked, and passed down these wonderful herding dog breeds to us. Without the development of herding dogs to help move livestock effectively and efficiently, it is possible that life for people could have developed very differently, and the opportunity to write this book might never have existed.

# Introduction

*You can know the name of a bird in all the languages of the world, but when you're finished, you'll know absolutely nothing whatever about the bird....So let's look at the bird and see what it's doing—that's what counts. I learned very early the difference between knowing the name of something and knowing something.*

*Richard Feynman, American physicist*

The notion that different dog breeds behave differently is not a new one. This is why so many different dog breeds exist in the first place. If people wanted or needed all dogs to look and behave exactly the same, countless thousands of people over the centuries would not have spent their time and resources to create the diversity of dog breeds alive today. But the obvious physical and behavioral differences that exist between breeds are often lost in the one-size-fits-all training approach applied in far too many traditional training classes. Little or no time is spent helping owners understand how their dogs' behaviors may be related, at least in part, to their breed instincts. As a result, many owners never truly understand the dogs looking back at them from the other end of the leash. This lack of understanding can lead to unrealistic behavioral expectations, ineffective training efforts, and unnecessary frustration. Helping owners understand and appreciate the breed they own will empower them to become better trainers and problem solvers. Ultimately, this should keep more herding dogs out of shelters and rescue groups and with families where they are loved and appreciated for what they are at heart.

While the breed-centric premise of this book is not new, the combination of exercises and their applications to life with a herding dog will provide you, a current or prospective herding dog owner, with effective breed-based approaches to changing your dog's unacceptable behaviors into more acceptable ones. This is not a book about teaching your dog basic obedience skills, such as sitting on cue. There are already many excellent books available that cover the mechanics of teaching these skills to any breed of dog. The Resources section at the end of this book lists several you may find helpful. This is not a book about training your dog to herd livestock, either. For dog owners who want to teach their herding dogs to herd, seeking out an experienced herding instructor is the best way to proceed. Training a working herding dog requires you to understand not only your dog, but also the livestock you are working with. Consulting with an instructor is the safest way for you to learn about both. *This* book gives you training exercises, management techniques, and games designed to address the unique training challenges that often come with opening your heart and home to a herding dog, particularly when you live in an urban environment.

Even though most people think of their dogs as family members, it is important to remember that no matter how much you love your dog, he is still a dog, not a furry little human. He is a beautiful, fascinating, intelligent, funny, irritating, independent, loyal, loving, hard-working, entertaining, unique being, but he is definitely *not* a human. He is a *dog*. And he is not just any type of dog, either; he is a *herding dog*. But he isn't Lassie or Rin Tin Tin reincarnated. Real herding dogs are even more amazing.

Once you understand and appreciate the similarities and differences between humans and dogs—and between herding dogs and other types of dogs—you can create a more positive relationship with your dog and you can effectively teach your dog how you expect him to behave in your home. This book will help you develop a loving, positive working relationship with your canine companion by teaching you how to work *with* your herding dog's instincts, rather than *against* them, to help him learn how to become an exceptional canine member of your family.

The book begins by exploring how modern herding dog breeds came into being and how the herding dog's ancestral work still affects behavior today. A brief introduction to basic canine learning theory and how to select meaningful reinforcers for your dog are also covered. The remainder of the book is devoted to what you need to teach your herding dog so he can successfully live in a world without livestock. Although you can certainly skip the history and theory chapters and jump right into the training exercises, you will be doing yourself and your dog a disservice if you do. The more you know about herding dogs and how they learn, the more effective you will be as a trainer and problem solver, and the more fulfilling your relationship with your dog will be. By developing a herding dog-centric view of the world, you can better help your herding dog reach his full potential as a family companion.

A brief note to those who have read *Terrier-Centric Dog Training: From Tenacious to Tremendous* or *From Birdbrained to Brilliant: Teaching the Sporting Dog to Be a Great Companion*: you may notice some repetition of management techniques and exercises between those books and this one. Basic management techniques are useful for dogs of any breed, but the reason for using a particular technique often varies considerably from breed to breed. For example, Respect the Bubble is a simple, effective management technique for a dog who tries to interact with other dogs while you are out walking together. You simply keep enough distance between the two dogs to prevent any physical interaction from happening in the first place. This technique works for any dog, of any breed.

The *type* of physical interaction you are trying to prevent varies considerably between different types of dogs. Herding dogs were developed to control the motion of other animals; an encounter between a herding dog and a dog he does not know, particularly one who is trying to be overly friendly or is moving erratically, may trigger those controlling instincts. If the other dog refuses to be controlled, the situation may quickly escalate to physical contact and quite possibly a fight. Sporting dogs were developed to work closely with humans and other dogs; a sporting dog who gets too close to another dog may try to kill the other dog with kindness by jumping on him, whining, and groveling for attention. This too may trigger a fight: if the sporting dog does not respond appropriately to cues from the other dog to back off, the dog being greeted may lash out in an attempt to stop all the goofy nonsense. Working terrier breeds were all developed to kill other animals. Inappropriate or unwanted interaction between a working terrier and another dog can trigger those killing instincts and the situation will likely escalate into a fight. In each case, if the dogs are kept at an appropriate distance from other dogs, again no unpleasant interactions or fights can ever occur between them. Three very different types of dogs, with three very different reasons to keep plenty of distance between them and other dogs when you are out for a walk, all helped by the same management technique.

Although there is definitely some overlap between the books, there are also several unique exercises included in this book designed to help you address herding dog-specific behaviors. And it is to better understanding your herding dog's instincts, and how to work with those instincts to help *your* herding dog become the exceptional companion he can be, that the rest of this book is devoted.

*Learning as much as you can about the history of herding dogs, their instincts, and how dogs learn will help you become a far more effective trainer.*

# Chapter 1

# What Exactly Is a Herding Dog?

*Without the shepherd's dog, the whole of the open mountainous land in Scotland would not be worth a sixpence. It would require more hands to manage a flock of sheep, gather them from the hills, force them into houses and folds, drive them to market, than the profits of the whole stock would be capable of maintaining.*

*James Hogg, aka the Ettrick Shepherd*
*Scottish poet and novelist*

People and dogs have been living and working together for thousands of years. While scientists continue to debate exactly when, how, and why domestic dogs first came into existence, they all agree the relationship benefited both. Soon after dogs were domesticated, people began to develop different types of dogs to perform specialized tasks to help humankind survive and thrive throughout the world. Herding dogs were developed to control the movement of herd animals, which improved people's ability to raise animals for food and clothing. The dog you own today still possesses most of the carefully selected physical traits and instincts of his working ancestors. These instincts influence his behavior, whether or not he actually performs any historical jobs associated with his breed. Understanding the history behind the development of the herding breeds is the first step toward developing a herding dog-centric training program that will help you train your dog in a positive, effective, fun way for both of you.

## Herding dog history in a nutshell

Domestication of herd animals profoundly influenced the development of human societies. Researchers generally concur that domestication of such animals began around 10,000 BCE in the Middle East. It is reasonable to assume that at about the same time, humans also began to develop dogs who could help them protect and manage their growing flocks and herds. Livestock guardian dogs were developed to protect flocks from wolves, lions, and other local predators. These dogs were big, fierce, usually white or light-colored, and protected their flock instinctively with little or no human direction or intervention. With the help of these dogs, larger herds and flocks could be protected with less human effort.

But another type of dog was needed to help control and move the ever-increasing size and number of herds and flocks. These dogs were typically smaller and more agile than the guardian breeds and were developed to meet specific local agrarian demands. As early as 3000 BCE, Sumerians were engaged extensively in both agriculture and trade and, according to Maxwell Riddle in *Dogs Through History*, used dogs for both guarding and herding purposes. Likewise, the ancient Egyptians and Greeks raised livestock and used dogs to help protect and move their flocks. A dog that distinctly resembled a type of collie dog was described in the Roman book *De Re Rustica* written in 36 BCE.

Unfortunately, early history of the development and use of herding dogs is rather scant compared to the information available about many of the breeds typically favored by nobility throughout the world. This paucity of information regarding early herding dogs reflects the low social status herdsmen occupied in most societies. These people were generally illiterate and considered too lowly to have details of their everyday lives, and the lives of their dogs, recorded in any permanent manner. Nevertheless, some societies did put legal value on working dogs, in recognition of the important work those dogs did. Tenth-century Welsh king Howel the Good, after seeing an early Border Collie-type dog working, imposed a scale of fines for killing a dog based on the maturity and training of the dog and the social status of the owner. Any shepherd dog owned by a *villein* (a partially free man under Welsh feudal law) was assessed "at sixty pence [the same as a nobleman's untrained buckhound] if the owners and one neighbor from each side could certify that it [the dog] led the herd out in the morning, brought them home in the evening, and made three turns around them in the night." Throughout the 1700s in Great Britain the privilege of owning a dog carried a heavy taxation burden, a shepherd's dog working on a farm was exempt from taxation. Initially the exemption applied only to those dogs whose tails were docked, because, as Stonehenge points out in his book *The Dog in Health and Disease*, "[It was] supposed that no one would keep a mutilated dog for anything but real service." Many early herding dogs had their tails docked, but when the taxation scheme was eventually altered to include all dogs, regardless of use, docking tails no longer served a purpose and most herding dogs were no longer docked.

The 1486 *Boke of St. Albans* by Dame Juliana Berners contains descriptions of two different types of herding dogs: "tryndel tayles" or long-tailed shepherd's dogs; and bob-tailed curs, which were used as drovers. By the time Johannes Cauis wrote *Of English Dogs* in 1576, herding dogs were of sufficient usefulness and necessity in Britain that he mentioned the shepherd dog in considerable detail; the dog he described is very similar to a modern-day working Border Collie. As agricultural practices continued to change, breeds were developed to move and control many different types of livestock, including sheep, cattle, geese, ostriches, goats, and pigs. By the early 1800's, nearly all the modern herding breeds were established.

Competitions to highlight herding dog speed and skill were incorporated into agricultural shows and fairs, particularly in Great Britain, as early as the late 1800's. The first recorded sheepdog trial was held in Bala, Wales, in 1873. Dogs were required to maneuver flocks over various courses, and prizes were usually given to the owners of the dogs who penned their sheep in the shortest amount of time. Competitions continue to be held throughout the world to allow owners to demonstrate the skills of their herding dogs.

The creation of the Kennel Club in Great Britain at about the same time, and with it the introduction of conformation shows, led to the rise in popularity of many herding dog breeds as pets among Victorian dog fanciers who had no need for working dogs. Differences in physical appearance between working lines and show lines started to develop in the more popular herding breeds, but all herding dogs retained the working instincts of their ancestors to some degree, regardless of their pedigrees.

*As conformation shows began to rise in popularity, so did the keeping of herding dogs strictly as non-working family companions.*

In the early 1900's, many traditional herding breeds, such as the German Shepherd Dog, the Belgian Shepherd, the Border Collie, and many of the all-around farm dog breeds, including the Airedale Terrier, were pressed into military service for World War I. These dogs served as Red Cross scouts, locating injured soldiers on the battlefield. They also served as messenger dogs, moving valuable information between military units, and guard dogs, protecting men and materiel from the enemy. German Shepherd Dogs starting seeing duty as guide dogs for the visually impaired at about the same time.

*Many different types of herding dogs were recruited into the
fledgling military canine corps during World War I.*

Herding dogs in the twenty-first century are still used the world over to move live-stock, assist military and police forces, and help the disabled. Along with the Belgian Malinois and a few other herding breeds, they continue to be used for military and police work, while many more herding breeds can be found working in non-herding jobs, including work as service dogs. However, as dog shows and canine media stars boosted herding dog popularity over the years, more people began to welcome them into their homes simply as pets. The herding dogs who participate in competitive dog sports, such as agility or herding trials, still "work hard," but their lifestyles are much different than that of their ancestors. Most modern herding dogs only "work" solely as family companions, a trend that began about a hundred years ago.

## How the work shaped the dog

Herding breeds have been specialized over the centuries to perform their work with livestock in several different ways. In her article *Tending the Flock*, Linda Rorem de-scribes the historical use of dogs as guardians and herders in various parts of the world. The exact type of work dogs did varied considerably, depending on the particular livestock involved, the terrain, and the way humans traditionally worked the livestock themselves. Most people think herding dogs are used only to control cattle or sheep, but they have also been used with other types of livestock when situations warranted it. Capt. Max von Stephanitz described the use of early German Shepherd Dogs by gosherds in eastern Germany to tend large flocks of geese: "The dog for such work must be carefully selected, for a goose is very short-tempered and has a very good idea about how to use its beak, but it cannot stand any grip. In former times when the geese in large flocks waddled from Posen to the Berlin market, shepherd dogs generally trotted along with them to drive them." Additionally, farmers often combined sheep, goats, and occasionally cattle, together into one flock and used dogs to assist in the movement of the flocks from pasture to pasture.

Once in the grazing area, the amount and type of work required from the dog primarily depended on the amount of crops in the vicinity. In highly cultivated areas, shepherds sometimes used more than one dog to actively patrol livestock to keep them out of other farmers' crop fields. This type of boundary work was common for French herding dogs, such as the Briard and the Berger Picard, since many areas of France were heavily cultivated. Von Stephanitz noted German agricultural conditions necessitated the use of dogs who patrolled the edges of grazing areas to keep livestock from trespassing on neighboring crops; shepherds could be fined for damage to crops done by their sheep. German Shepherd Dogs proved particularly valuable in this type of work. Flocks had to be kept in the grass plots between the main roads and away from nearby grain fields. Shepherds with access to larger grazing areas sometimes practiced "grazing in the square." One section of a pasture would be completely grazed down, then the flock would be moved to another area, allowing the grazed-down land to recover. Dogs were used to keep the sheep in particular sections of the pasture so the long-term health of the vegetation could be better maintained. Herding dogs with less ability for patrolling boundaries could be used successfully in less-populated or less-cultivated areas such as Scotland. Dogs were also invaluable in the seasonal transhumances, helping herdsmen move their livestock between fixed summer and winter pastures at differing elevations throughout a large part of Europe and the Middle East. This migration required dogs who could control motion and, if need be, move flocks over long distances in a relatively short amount of time.

Tradition also played a role in the development of particular canine herding styles. For example, continental European shepherds usually led their flocks, while British and American shepherds usually walked behind the flocks. Local needs created variations in practices. Shepherds in southern Germany often walked along side their flocks, toward the middle of the group, while Low Country shepherds moving smaller flocks could be seen walking among the sheep. Dogs needed to have complementary herding styles to accommodate local human practices. But regardless of the dog's position relative to the shepherd and flock, his primary job was to control the speed and direction of the flock's movement, and he maneuvered around the flock as required to accomplish his task.

SHEPHERDS OF THE LANDES.—[SEE PAGE 350.]

*Local shepherd customs, including the use of stilts, influenced
herding dog breed development throughout the world.*

## Headers, heelers, and just about everything in between

There are several ways to categorize modern herding dog breeds. One common way is by how they typically herd livestock. Behaviors associated with various herding breeds can be described based on which end of the livestock the dog focuses on to control the animal (headers and heelers), or how the livestock is moved (drivers, tenders, and gatherers). Well-trained, experienced herding dogs often show a combination of herding behaviors, depending on circumstances, but one style of control and movement tends to show up more than others in any given herding breed.

Probably the best know header breed is the Border Collie. This dog was developed to quietly and quickly gather flocks across the rugged Scottish countryside. Prior to

World War I, these working dogs were referred to simply as "collies," but with the rising popularity of dog shows, several types of collies were developed in both the UK and the United States. Border Collies differ from the others in that they work primarily along the sides and at the front of the flock or herd, controlling motion by "giving eye" (staring) to exert psychological pressure on the livestock. Border Collies usually don't resort to "gripping" (biting) to move animals, because sheep have relatively thin skin and would be injured if controlled primarily by biting. These dogs also have a unique "crouch" they exhibit when herding; head low, hindquarters high, and tail down allows these dogs to strongly convey predatory movements to control the flock. Border Collies are keenly aware of "balance point," which refers to the distance they need to maintain between themselves and the sheep to keep them from fleeing haphazardly. This awareness, coupled with their agility and intelligence, has made them extremely specialized for use with sheep, particularly when the terrain is challenging and dogs are required to work at considerable distances from the shepherds. Header breeds are also used as gatherers to bring separate animals together into a group that is then moved around as a single unit.

*An early illustration of a Border Collie, one of the best known header breeds.*

Australian Cattle Dogs (also known as Blue Heelers and Red Heelers), Cardigan Welsh Corgis, and Pembroke Welsh Corgis are three of the better-known heeler breeds. Heeler breeds rely more on physical contact and nipping at hind legs than the header breeds do to move livestock and are usually employed to move cattle. Heelers move livestock by driving them from behind, moving them away from the herder. Many heeler breeds are fairly short and stout in stature; this physical build allows them to better avoid being kicked by cows, and increases their chances of survival if they are kicked.

*The short, athletic build of the Cardigan Welsh Corgi*
*makes it well suited for working with cattle.*

Two Australian herding breeds, the Kelpie and the Koolie, are examples of dogs that work as head, heel, and back dogs. They naturally move between nipping from behind, eyeing from the front, and, if the situation warrants, actually jumping on the backs of livestock to keep them moving in the correct direction. Although most herding breeds will switch between these activities if the situation warrants, acting from all angles to move livestock comes very naturally to head, heel, and back breeds.

German Shepherd Dogs, Beaucerons, and Berger Picards are three of the many breeds developed to work as a "living fence," tending to flocks and herds by running the perimeters to keep them off roads and out of nearby fields as they move from place to place. Rather than moving a herd from one location to another, these dogs are taught to keep the herd within a defined area. According to herdingdogsontheweb. com, "Dogs who have been bred with an emphasis on boundary work tend to be very keen, active dogs. They are readily guided into moving along a demarcated field edge, roadside, etc., to keep the flock contained. Those that have strong boundary instincts will, with experience, pick up very subtle boundaries and can even make their own when shown a line to take—they will go out the indicated direction, return along the same line, and then continue patrolling on that path."

*The German Shepherd often acted as a "living fence" to keep livestock in a defined area.*

Regardless of the specific methods employed to move and confine livestock, all herding dogs share a unique set of instincts that help them effectively and efficiently control the movement of other animals. Understanding these instincts will help you better understand your herding dog's behavior. The next two chapters will look at these herding traits in greater detail.

## Herding dogs vs. livestock guardian dogs

The management techniques and training exercises in this book can be used with any dog, but they were specifically selected for herding dog breeds that were traditionally used under human direction to contain or move herds and flocks. The instincts modified in herding breeds vary in many important ways from the instincts modified and intensified in the livestock guardian breeds, such as Anatolian Shepherds, Kuvaszok, and Pyrenean Mastiffs. These breeds were used mainly to protect livestock from predators, often with little human assistance, rather than actually control or move them. Livestock guardian breeds share more instincts in common with mastiffs and other breeds developed primarily as guard dogs than with the herding breeds, and are therefore not discussed in detail in this book. See the Appendix for a list of the herding dog breeds that are the focus of the management techniques and training exercises contained in later chapters.

# Chapter 2

## Why Should I Care Which Breed of Dog I Own? Dogs Are Dogs, Right?

---

*Ay, in the catalogue ye go for men;*
*As hounds, and greyhounds, mongrels, spaniels, curs,*
*Shoughs, water-rugs, and demi-wolves, are 'clept*
*All by the name of dogs: the valued file*
*Distinguishes the swift, the slow, the subtle,*
*The housekeeper, the hunter, every one*
*According to the gift which bounteous nature*
*Hath in him closed.*

*William Shakespeare*
*Macbeth*

For most owners, the decision to open our hearts and homes to a herding dog has little or nothing to do with needing canine help to herd livestock. There is something magnetic about these breeds. Herding dogs have been portrayed for decades as having near-human intelligence and being capable of fantastic problem-solving exploits and physical feats. Generations have been entertained by their beauty and intelligence, through books, movies, and television. The Collie Lassie and German Shepherd Dogs Strongheart and Rin Tin Tin captivated people with their valiant acts on the radio and television, and in books and movies, for years. The Walt Disney movie *The Shaggy Dog* made many fall in love with the rugged good looks of the Old English Sheepdog. More recently, the movie *Because of Winn-Dixie* introduced a relatively rare herding breed, the Berger Picard, to potential dog owners. Border Collies with human qualities appeared in the *Babe* movies, as well as in *Angel Dog*. News coverage of the real-life heroism of police and military dogs continues to draw attention to Belgian Malinois, German Shepherd Dogs, and Rottweilers. People watch herding breeds, including Shetland Sheepdogs, Australian Shepherds, and Border Collies, compete in televised agility trials, flyball tournaments, and conformation shows. Herding dogs are amazing dogs, captured in the media doing amazing things. For some first-time herding dog owners, that sensational media presentation directly led to their decision to bring a herding dog home.

But many first-time owners are not prepared for the work it takes to live successfully with a herding dog, particularly in an urban environment. Whether consciously or subconsciously, owners sometimes believe these dogs can learn and reason just like humans, and therefore require little or no training and will behave just like Lassie! But herding dogs are dogs. Even though they are extremely smart, they don't think or reason exactly like humans do. And they are not born knowing how to behave in a human world; they are born only knowing how to behave in a canine world. It is up to you to teach your dog how to behave in your world.

In some ways, herding dogs require even more work than other types of dogs if they are to become enjoyable pets. In addition to the extreme amounts of exercise most of them need in order to be physically healthy, these dogs constantly need training and work to do to be mentally healthy and happy living in an urban environment. If you have realistic expectations about the amount of time and effort it will take to keep a herding dog in your home, if you understand and respect your dog's herding instincts and how those instincts affect his behavior in the real world, and if you are committed to doing the necessary work with your dog, you will have a willing, eager, and capable canine student who will gladly work hard to learn all the lessons you choose to teach him. You will also be able to provide your dog the type of training he needs to rival any dog, real or fictional, as an exceptional family member.

## How instincts influence behavior

Many elements influence your dog's behavior. Canid and breed-specific instincts, his experiences and unique personality, his physical and mental health, and your skill and efforts as a trainer all combine to make your dog different from any other who has ever existed. Some of these elements, such as the experiences and the training you provide him, are directly under your control. Other elements, like breed instincts, are not directly under your control. You can certainly influence when and how your dog expresses his instincts, but you can never completely eliminate them. Those instincts form the basic outline of your dog's behavior, like the outline of a picture in a child's coloring book: experiences, training, health, and individual attributes are the color and texture placed inside that outline to create a one-of-a-kind work of art. You may be able to slightly enlarge or shrink his individual behavioral outline, but no matter what you do, the basic outline will remain the same. Moreover, every breed has its own unique behavioral outline, determined by the type of work the breed was developed to perform. The variations between breed outlines will always remain, regardless of the amount of training you do.

Although every dog is a unique individual, breeds developed to perform similar tasks tend to share more physical and behavioral traits in common with each other than with dogs developed to perform different types of tasks. While herding styles may vary, breeds developed to herd animals all perform the same basic task of controlling the motion of livestock. Similarly, breeds developed to eradicate vermin share characteristics that facilitate killing other animals, and breeds developed to hunt alongside humans share certain characteristics that allow them to effectively locate and bring back game. Herding dogs share more specific behavioral traits with each other than they do with terriers or sporting dogs. It isn't realistic or productive to expect a herding dog to ever behave the same as a terrier or sporting dog and training a herding dog isn't exactly the same as training any other type of dog. Your dog's breed instincts will likely determine the most effective way for you to teach, reward, and maintain trained behaviors.

*Every breed of dog has a behavioral "outline" which you can never eliminate completely. The training you give him and the environment in which he lives can shape a somewhat unique personality for the dog, but there are limits to how much his breed instincts can be altered.*

## One size rarely fits all

The popularity of sporting dogs, such as Golden and Labrador Retrievers, as family pets skews many training classes understandably toward training techniques and rewards that are most effective with these types of dogs. This bias may make the most sense from a business perspective, but training approaches tailored to those breeds (who generally respond willingly to human direction) are not always the most effective and efficient way to train other types of dogs. Let's compare three very different types of dogs to see why that is usually the case. The Border Collie, the Jack Russell Terrier, and the Curly-Coated Retriever are three British-refined breeds who, for generations, earned their keep by performing important work for their owners. They are physically and mentally tough dogs, known for having high pain tolerance, and have the ability to stay focused on a task for a long period of time. To varying degrees, each breed performed its work with little or no direct physical help from people.

*Gabriel stands ready to herd.*

The Border Collie was developed to move flocks of sheep over hazardous terrain with minimal direction or physical assistance from the shepherd. The instincts and intelligence necessary for this type of work give Border Collies the reputation of being the "smartest" of all dog breeds. History is full of fantastic accounts of Border Collies achieving amazing feats of mental and physical skill.

The Jack Russell Terrier was developed for use during fox hunts: these dogs forced foxes out of their underground refuges so they could be hunted by the hound pack. Famous for their tenacity and single-minded determination to complete this underground task, these terriers were also highly valued by those in need of general vermin exterminators on farms and in homes. Cleverness is a key characteristic of the breed.

*Lizzie B. can't wait to be released to begin hunting at an AKC earthdog test.*

The Curly-Coated Retriever was developed to locate and retrieve shot wildfowl, often from extremely frigid waters. They were known as the premier "meat dog" for gamekeepers and poachers alike due to their intelligence, tenacity, and ability to locate downed birds by scent. The American Kennel Club breed standard refers to Curlys as "wickedly smart."

*Eli is a useful hunting companion, both in and out of the water.*

Looking at the jobs performed by these three breeds, all clearly require dogs who exhibited intelligence, physical strength, courage, independence, and endurance. These general attributes create broad behavioral similarities between the three breeds. However, the job each breed historically performed also required unique skills. Although these three breeds have many characteristics in common, they also differ in many significant ways that are important to take into consideration when training.

The primary behavior chain that was altered, through selective breeding, to develop these three breeds was the basic predatory behavior chain dogs inherited from their wild ancestors. To be a successful hunter, a canid predator must carry out a series of behaviors, namely, eye–stalk–chase–grab–shake–kill–eat–guard carcass remains. For example, a wolf first locates his prey by using his eyesight, sense of smell, and hearing. Once he has found it, the wolf will watch and then start slowly stalking his prey. When the animal begins to run, the wolf chases; when larger prey animals are involved, the chase is often a shared activity between members of the pack. The kill is usually accomplished by a bite to the neck, followed by a series of violent shakes that breaks the prey's spine or neck, and then the feast begins. Carcass remnants are sometimes guarded if the entire animal isn't consumed in one meal. This is the basic behavior chain that was modified in different ways to create herding dogs, terriers, and sporting dogs.

Shepherds are able to use Border Collies to herd livestock because prey animals instinctively avoid predators, while simultaneously trying to maintain the integrity of their flock or herd. From a sheep's point of view, a herding dog is simply a wolf in dog's clothing; the sheep has no idea the dog will not actually kill him. Herding is an elaborate dance between predator (dog) and prey (sheep) that has been choreographed by carefully altering the basic predatory behavior chain in herding dog breeds to prevent the dance from ending with the death and consumption of one of the flock. Through generations of selective breeding, Border Collies were developed to have extremely strong eye, stalk, and chase behaviors. By contrast the grab, shake, kill, eat, and guard portions of the predatory behavior chain were intentionally weakened. Careful training further refines the dog's instinctive behaviors and places them under the shepherd's control. It is pointless to have a herding dog who kills the very animals he is supposed to be herding, or who won't move a flock as directed by the shepherd.

*From a sheep's point of view, Gabriel is a black-and-white wolf.*

Although the shepherd may give his Border Collie directions, an independent nature and exceptional problem-solving skills are genetically hard-wired into Border Collies to help them appropriately interact with livestock with minimal human assistance. Border Collies tend to be indifferent or aloof to people they don't know, and often prefer work to play. High energy levels are also the norm for this breed. Herding work is physically demanding, and dogs must have the strength and stamina to do their work day after day. All of these characteristics combine to form the foundation of the controlling "herding personality" that is common in most Border Collies. Because of these instincts, most Border Collies must be taught to resist the urge to control everything that moves (including, but certainly not limited to, people, cars, and cats), to take direction from their owners, and to stop working when told to quit.

Working terrier breeds were originally developed to locate and harass or kill some type of vermin, ranging in size from mice to badgers and otters. Only the last two steps in the predatory behavior chain—namely, eating and guarding—have been significantly altered in these breeds. Working terriers had to locate, stalk, chase, grab, shake, and harass or kill vermin, then willingly leave the prey alone once it died (or quit moving). Terriers were bred to move quickly, bite decisively and lethally, and shake prey to kill quickly and efficiently; those dogs that moved slowly or hesitated when going for the kill were often hurt or killed themselves, removing them from the gene pool. "Giving voice" (barking) was another trait specifically enhanced in terriers used to work quarry underground. Although outright aggression toward other dogs was never desired, most early terriers worked alone and did not necessarily need to get along with other dogs to do their daily work.

*The only thing deterring Glitch from going to ground to explore an animal's den is his leash.*

This slightly truncated predatory behavior chain, present in all working terrier breeds, is particularly well preserved in Jack Russell Terriers. The hard-wired behaviors common in the Jack Russell Terrier often result in dogs who are quite vocal when excited, and make them willing to chase, harass, and quite possibly kill, without hesitation, anything that moves. This includes cats, birds, and squeaky toys. Jacks sometimes "bite first, ask questions later" when overstimulated. They are notorious for not getting along well with other dogs, even those they have lived with all their lives. They are independent thinkers and actors. Combined with intrinsically high energy levels and tenacity, these hard-wired traits can be very problematic if they aren't channeled into more appropriate behaviors. Together, these instincts produce the feisty, tenacious, vocal "terrier personality" and explain why terriers often must be taught to work cooperatively with their owners, tolerate the presence of other dogs, and resist the urge to chase and grab anything that moves too quickly.

Developing a dog to help locate and retrieve game required slightly different manipulations of the predatory behavior chain than those used to develop herding or terrier breeds. The predatory instincts to shake, kill, eat, and guard were modified in the Curly-Coated Retriever to produce a dog that, with proper training, would watch game as it fell after being shot, chase it if it was merely wounded and could still run, grab it, and then return it back to his handler without damaging or eating it. A retriever must grasp birds firmly but gently to return them to the hunter intact, so a "soft mouth" is required; the shake-kill-eat-guard part of the predatory chain has been greatly diminished. Retrievers must also be quiet when working, since unnecessary barking in the field could scare game beyond firing range. Hunters sometimes work more than one dog at a time and may hunt out of small blinds or boats with other hunters, so retrievers must be comfortable spending long periods of time in close proximity to other dogs and working with them.

The behaviors genetically hard-wired in a Curly-Coated Retriever combine to form the foundation of the hard working, willing-to-please "retriever personality" that makes retriever breeds so popular as family pets. These retriever instincts result in dogs who readily accept direction from people ("biddability") and will tolerate a certain amount of repetitious training because of their strong desire to work under the direction of their owners. They may need to be taught self-control around people and other dogs, and to accept being left alone.

By manipulating the basic canid predatory behavior chain in three different ways over generations of selective breeding, three unique breeds were created to help man perform three very different tasks. These refined instincts still exist in our present-day dogs, even though most Border Collies no longer herd sheep, most Jack Russell Terriers no longer go to ground after foxes or kill rats, and most Curly-Coated Retrievers no longer retrieve game. Instinctive differences are the reason a herding dog doesn't act the same as a terrier or sporting dog (or any other type of dog, for that matter) and why you can never train your herding dog to act exactly like the Jack Russell Terrier you owned as a child or the Curly-Coated Retriever next door. The only way to have a dog who behaves like a typical Jack Russell Terrier or a Curly-Coated Retriever is to have a Jack Russell Terrier or a Curly-Coated Retriever in the first place. These instinctual differences are also why training techniques and rewards developed to work well for sporting dogs or terriers might not be the most effective ones to use with your herding dog.

*Although Gabriel and Lizzie share many instincts and have been taught many of the same behaviors, they will always be very different types of dogs at heart.*

## The power of herding dog-centric training

The power of herding dog-centric training lies in understanding the very essence of the herding dog you have brought into your home and appreciating your herding dog for what he is, rather than trying to make him into something he isn't. This does not mean that you should use the fact that he is a herding dog to excuse, justify, or abide unsafe or unacceptable behaviors. However, understanding herding dog instincts is the key to developing a proactive, effective training plan for reaching any realistic goal you set for your herding dog. The next chapter will look at these instincts in even greater detail.

*By working with, rather than against, the herding instincts Dutch Shepherd Zen has, Gloria will be able to help her dog become a truly exceptional canine companion.*

# Chapter 3

# What Are Typical
# Herding Dog Traits?

*Utility is the true criterion of beauty.*

*Max von Stephanitz*
*German Shepherd Dog expert*

Herding dogs share several behavioral traits. Understanding these traits will help you understand your dog better. However, your dog might not exhibit all of these common herding dog traits all the time. In fact, he might not show some of these traits at all. These typical traits are a combination of the instincts herding dogs inherit from their herding ancestors and the unique learned behaviors they acquire. Dogs are thinking, feeling individuals, so no one can ever say with 100% certainty how a particular dog will behave, based strictly on what is considered "normal" breed behavior. But it's a safe bet your herding dog has shown you or will show you at least a few of these traits at some point in his life. If you understand the behavioral traits you might see in your herding dog, you will be better equipped to address those traits if, or when, they show up.

## No-nonsense attitude

Herding dogs are, first and foremost, working dogs. These breeds were not developed as companion dogs, but as working tools, used to accomplish difficult farm work. Most have little or no tolerance for excessive goofiness or senseless motion from other animals or people. Panmure Gordon, quoted in W. D. Drury's *British Dogs*, describes the general character of the Collie as "the reverse of treacherous, although he is not so ready to bestow his confidence in a 'love-at-first-sight' way, as some breeds that are accustomed to fawn and to be fondled are. His affections, once placed, are strong and his memory tenacious; and these qualities, combined with his unusually high intelligence, make him one of the most interesting and pleasant of companions." Even those dogs who enjoy lounging on the sofa all day are generally quite serious when asked to work. Herding dog puppies often stop playing rough-and-tumble puppy games and start practicing more specific herding behaviors at a very young age. Adult herding dogs usually prefer the company of their owners and, perhaps, a select few other dogs, to the company of strangers or strange dogs. The very act of working, whether it is performing a simple obedience task or actually herding livestock, can be a powerful motivator for herding dogs.

## The urge to take control

Herding dogs are also control freaks, a trait which can lead to problem behaviors such as chasing and barking. If there is *anything* in motion around a herding dog, he may feel the instinctual need to control it in some manner. Herding involves circling and chasing animals to keep them in a group and moving in the "correct" direction. If an individual animal is being defiant or difficult to move, a herding dog may resort to barking, nipping, or biting to get the animal moving. These are the same default behaviors he will use any time he tries to herd a moving object, no matter what that object is. "Farm dogs" (often herding breeds or herding breed mixes) occasionally get hurt or killed chasing cars the same way they would chase cattle. Many herding dogs who end up in shelters are surrendered for biting children or other animals the same way they might bite uncontrollable livestock. It is a far too common sight at agility trials and flyball tournaments to see herding dogs, particularly Border Collies, barking at the top of their lungs in frustration because they can't stop all the motion as they watch other dogs running and jumping. Herding dogs are fun police *extraordinaire*— if something moves too much, it needs to be controlled. And a herding dog is just the dog to assume responsibility for controlling it.

## Low frustration threshold

It can take relatively little stimulation to frustrate a herding dog. Controlling large animals requires dogs who are aware of the slightest motion in the herd and who act accordingly, before the situation gets out of hand. A herding dog can become quite frustrated if his efforts to control a situation aren't successful or if he isn't allowed to take control in the first place. Once he is frustrated, it becomes difficult for him to listen to you or learn what you are trying to teach him. Signs that a herding dog is potentially frustrated or overly excited include uncontrollable barking and spinning behaviors. Setting clear behavioral expectations for your herding dog and thinking through your training process *before* you actually work with him will help minimize frustration for both of you.

## Tenacity and focus

Herding dogs must be tenacious and focused on the job at hand to move livestock. Once a dog confronts an animal, he has to stand his ground and stick with his job, no matter how long it takes to get the animal to move in the correct direction. Recent studies suggest that some breeds, including Border Collies and Belgian Malinois, actually have more dopamine receptors in their brains than other breeds, which helps them engage in prolonged difficult tasks. British behaviorist Carol Price describes Border Collies as exhibiting what she calls "obsessionalism." She uses this term to describe the innate drive Border Collies have that pushes them to work harder and longer toward a goal than most other dogs would. This trait is very useful in working dogs, allowing them to stay focused on their livestock for hours, days, and even weeks at a time if necessary. But taken to the extreme, particularly in herding dogs who don't work livestock, obsessionalism can lead to abnormal, repetitive behaviors, resembling obsessive-compulsive behaviors in people. These dogs can chase a ball around the yard for hours on end, or chase their tails until they collapse. Tenacity, focus, and obsessionalism can be found, to some extent, in most other herding breeds as well. They can become difficult traits to live with if not channeled into appropriate behavior through effective management and training.

## Excessive barking

Some herding breeds were developed to be more vocal than others when working livestock. Dogs who relied, at least in part, on barking to move animals needed to be able to bark for long periods of time if the situation required them to do so. They also needed loud, piercing voices that would carry over the noise of the herd. Modern herding dogs still have the penetrating voices of their working ancestors and the ability to bark for extended periods of time. If a herding dog is bored or gets overly excited, he may launch into an annoying extended barking spree. Unfortunately, this is one behavior that can bother your neighbors as much as it bothers you. Consistent management and training are necessary to keep your dog's barking at an acceptable level.

## Exceptional energy

Herding dogs come from a long line of dogs bred to herd, run, swim, and boss other animals around on a daily basis; they have an innate need to be physically active. The amount of exercise the typical herding dog needs is phenomenal. Linda Rorem, in her Internet article *An Overview of Herding in France*, estimates that some dogs doing boundary/border work to keep sheep out of crop fields and within the proper grazing area might run fifty to fifty-five miles per day! During transhumance movements, dogs may run even farther on a daily basis when moving livestock between seasonal pastures located one hundred or more miles apart. The need for significant daily exercise is not a new revelation to dog owners. Writing in the 1800's, British dog fancier Hugh Dalziel noted, "All dogs should be regularly exercised; it is cruel to keep a dog on the chain or confined to house or kennel without relief or change; and the dog being naturally an active animal, when his exercise is prevented, illness almost surely follows. People who keep dogs, if obliged to keep them confined for the most part, should arrange for them to have at least one hour's exercise a day. Taking a pet dog out for a carriage airing is not a substitute." If you can't provide structured ways for your dog to satisfy his need for strenuous regular exercise, a herding dog is not the type of dog for you. And if you don't provide him enough exercise, he *will* come up with his own exercise routine, and the chances are very good that you won't like what he dreams up!

## Über-intelligence

Two common beliefs among many first-time herding dog owners are that (1) herding dogs are so smart they just "know" how to behave acceptably in any situation, without any training; and (2) when herding dogs don't behave appropriately, it is because they are stubborn or seeking revenge for some alleged wrong inflicted upon them by their owners minutes, hours, or days before. Of course, neither of these beliefs is true. Although herding dogs are known for their keen intelligence, they are born knowing only how to be dogs, with absolutely no understanding of what the rules are for dogs living in a human world. Without training, your herding dog only knows how to behave the way his instincts and personal experiences tell him to behave.

In his book *The Intelligence of Dogs*, researcher Stanley Coren divides canine intelligence into several categories, including working/obedience intelligence, adaptive intelligence, and instinctive intelligence. Working/obedience intelligence measures how well a dog will learn to perform commands and act under the direction of humans. Adaptive intelligence measures how well dogs problem solve and learn on their own. Instinctive intelligence focuses on the genetically determined behavioral predispositions that dogs inherit. In herding dogs, these would include circling, gripping, and other typical herding dog behaviors. Most herding breeds score well above average in working/obedience intelligence and adaptive intelligence measures and excel in the instinctive intelligence category. When all three measures are combined, herding dog breeds make up half of the top twenty-five on Coren's list of the "most intelligent" dog breeds popular today. Border Collies occupy the number one spot on this list. If necessary, herding dogs can work with little or no human direction, guided by strong herding instincts that have been carefully refined through training. Their overall intelligence makes them ideal dogs to undertake very complex tasks, in addition to herding, and is one reason why several herding breeds are popular with military and police forces and service dog organizations.

Herding dogs must have a job to do on a daily basis to stay mentally healthy. These breeds in addition to being intelligent are persistent and creative. If you don't give a herding dog an acceptable outlet for his instincts and energy, he will create one to occupy his time. The job you give him can be as simple as coming to you the first time you call him or as complex as moving a huge herd of cattle from pasture to pasture. Every behavior you teach your herding dog is a "job" you are asking him to do. The larger his repertoire of learned behaviors is, the more jobs he will have to do, and the more mentally healthy he will be. Just as the more physical exercise you give him, the physically healthier he will be. Owning a herding dog in an urban environment is definitely not for the faint of heart or those with sedentary lifestyles! Nor is it for anyone who won't commit to daily training and consistent behavioral expectations. Herding dogs are incredible companions who require an incredible amount of work. Knowing this before you get a herding dog, and respecting this after you get one, will help you and your dog develop a great working relationship that is happy and healthy for both of you.

## Normal isn't always acceptable

Although understanding breed instincts allows you to better grasp what "normal," instinct-based behavior is for your herding dog, normal behavior is *not* necessarily *acceptable* behavior. When a dog becomes overstimulated or stressed, his behaviors often reflect his breed instincts. For example, when a herding dog sees sheep for the first time, his normal instinctual urge may be to circle the sheep and try to control their motion. That is, after all, what herding dogs were developed to do. Depending on his breed, he may bark at the sheep or he may remain silent; he may approach from the front with a strong stare or come in from behind and start nipping. This is all perfectly normal behavior for a herding dog. Nevertheless, such uncontrolled instinctual behavior is not acceptable behavior in a herding dog kept as a family pet. Herding dogs aren't born knowing the differences between cattle, children, and cars. They need to be taught to ignore their herding instincts and not try to control moving people or vehicles. Herding dogs who bark, bite, and circle anything that moves are not abnormal, stubborn, or out of control. They are normal herding dogs, engaging in normal, instinctual herding dog behavior in an unacceptable manner. You will never completely extinguish those instincts, but you can definitely teach your dog to control them in most situations.

## Pulling it all together

So what does all this mean for a herding dog owner? It means a herding dog is generally a very willing and eager learner, with or without human guidance, who will demand considerable time and effort from you to adapt to a non-working life. You will have to take into account his intelligence, establish fair, consistent behavioral expectations, and take responsibility for teaching him how to behave in an acceptable way, if you want a dog you can live with in your home. Unacceptable behaviors do not happen because your dog is stubborn or spiteful. They happen because your herding dog is just what he is—a herding dog who needs to be taught how to behave in your home. You need to be realistic, patient, persistent, and consistent with your behavioral expectations and accept that while the instincts in every herding dog can be controlled, they will never be completely eliminated. Respect, relax, and enjoy that wonderful bundle of herding dog instincts you brought into your home. When you accept your herding dog for what he is, training him will become a positive, productive journey you take together, rather than an unpleasant regimen you inflict on your dog and yourself.

# Chapter 4

## Socialization, Puppy Classes, and a Word About Dog Parks

*A puppy is but a dog, plus high spirits, and minus common sense.*

*Agnes Repplier*
*American essayist*

Proper socialization and early training are two irreplaceable ingredients in the recipe for a happy, confident, socially appropriate adult herding dog. A dog's behavior is influenced by his genetic makeup and both the intentional and unintentional socialization experiences and training he receives. Puppy brains grow just like all the other parts of their bodies. Without proper environmental stimulation during the brain's growth period, the brain will not develop to its full potential. The stimulation and experiences you give your young herding dog should either enhance the herding instincts you want to increase in your dog or weaken those you want to decrease. Proper socialization and early puppy training will maximize your chances of having an adult herding dog you will enjoy living with for many years.

## Socialization is far more than just puppy play

In *The Dog Vinci Code*, well-known British canine behaviorist John Rogerson defines socialization as learning how to interact appropriately with people, other dogs, and the environment. Socialization involves exposing a puppy to as many things as possible during the first sixteen weeks of his life, before he develops a normal, healthy fear of new things. Your puppy needs to learn how to interact appropriately with other dogs, how to tolerate physical confinement and brief periods of isolation, how to ride in the car, how to abide being handled by you and other people, how to cope with unique environmental conditions where you live (such as neighborhood noises, sights, and smells), and how to deal with unique family situations (including babies, the elderly, medical equipment, and pets of other species). Every socialization experience should be short, pleasant, and puppy-appropriate, but the experiences should reflect the environment you expect your adult dog to live in and any work you might want him to do later in life. Investing the time and effort to socialize your puppy properly will result in huge benefits that will last your dog's entire lifetime.

Dogs don't always identify or respond to environmental stimuli the same way humans do. Canine instincts help a dog survive in the natural world, but sometimes cause problems in the human-made world. For example, dogs are naturally fearful of loud noises. In nature, such noises usually accompany dangerous things, such as lightning or a falling boulder. However, in the man-made world, there are loud things that are not necessarily dangerous, such as fireworks and garbage trucks. Dogs aren't born knowing the difference between dangerous loud things and not-so-dangerous loud things. They need to learn the distinction through socialization and experience. As behaviorist Carol Price explains: "Dogs…are essentially creatures of instinct…. This…in turn means that when a dog is suddenly faced with something strange—be it a sight, sound, object, person, animal or experiences—he has one of two choices. He can either inherently trust that something is safe, or fear that it is not—and then react accordingly." Providing as many appropriate, safe, novel socialization experiences for your puppy as you possibly can will help tip the scales toward an assumption that novel stimuli are safe. Your herding dog puppy also needs exposure to things that move quickly or erratically, such as bicycles, vacuum sweepers, and skateboards, so he can learn they are safe objects that don't need to be controlled.

*Socialization should begin long before you bring your puppy home. These six-week-old Shetland Sheepdog puppies from Dimar Kennel have a play box containing many unique items to explore and interact with in a safe environment.*

The same concept applies to developing proper canine social skills. Dogs have the instinctive ability to express themselves in ways that other dogs understand. However, if a dog is not given the opportunity to practice and refine those skills during the first sixteen weeks of his life, while his brain is still developing those areas associated with canine communication, his fluency will be greatly diminished. He may have problems throughout his life being socially appropriate with other dogs. He needs to be exposed to dogs of both sexes, different physical appearances (for example color, size, shape, coat length, head shape), different ages, and different inclinations toward interacting with puppies. It is vital your puppy interacts with dogs who will tell him to bug off (in a socially appropriate way, of course) so he learns that not every dog wants to play, or be herded, and how to stop potential conflicts from escalating. If your puppy grows up only interacting with other puppies or adult dogs who tolerate his herding behaviors, he may not act appropriately the first time he encounters a dog who wants to be left alone. Although it is very important that your dog learns how to interact with other dogs he lives with, he still needs the opportunity to interact with dogs outside his family. If he is limited to interacting only with the dogs he lives with, his communication skills will be limited by the degree of fluency his housemates have. He might also struggle with communicating with dogs you bring into your home in the future, if he doesn't learn how to communicate properly.

Play is another key part of socialization. Puppy play is Mother Nature's way of teaching puppies how to be predators (eye, stalk, chase, and grab skills are all part of typical puppy play) and how to communicate with one another (bite inhibition, social deference, and other skills also develop through play). Once puppies are four to six months old, these lessons are pretty much learned (or not learned, if the puppy wasn't adequately socialized) and the desire to play starts to naturally decline. Older puppies and adult dogs may still "play" with other dogs, but the nature and frequency of that play changes. As puppies mature, their extended chase, tumble, and chew games evolve into more casual shared environmental exploration. Unfortunately, adult herding dogs sometimes want to interact with other dogs by herding them. The innate need to control other animals can cause problems and trigger fights if your herding dog never learns that "no" means "no" when he is interacting with other dogs. That is why it is so important that herding puppies learn that not every dog they encounter wants to play a game of shepherd-and-sheep, and to respect that decision.

*As adults, Gabriel and Shishka enjoy exploring the
shore together, instead of rough-and-tumble play.*

Unfortunately, an intense period of fear development partially overlaps the optimal learning period for many critical adult behaviors; negative experiences during a fear period can last a lifetime. It is important to protect your puppy from traumatic experiences, while still providing him with positive ones. Throwing him into a mob scene with a pack of strange dogs at the dog park to socialize him is *not* a good idea. Chances are high that your puppy will be scared by such an experience, and this can greatly impair his social skill development. It is far safer to have your young puppy interact with a few other socially appropriate dogs under the supervision of a trainer in a controlled environment, such as training class, than to toss him out to fend for himself in the dog park. Although this requires more effort on your part, remember that you are creating a behavioral foundation that will last your dog's entire life and you only have a few months to get most of that foundation laid.

# Puppy classes

One significant mistake many herding dog owners make with their dogs is to wait too long to begin socialization and training. Puppies start learning from the moment they are born. The longer you wait to begin teaching your puppy how you expect him to behave in your family, the more difficult your task will be. Puppies do what comes naturally to them and what gets them what they want or need. Many times these normal puppy behaviors are in direct conflict with what owners want or expect from their dogs. Training needs to be adjusted to take into account your puppy's age, but the earlier his training begins, the sooner your puppy will begin to understand what you expect of him and how he should behave.

The most important training class you will ever select for your herding dog is his early puppy class. Ideally, the puppy class you choose will place plenty of emphasis on having puppies interact with other dogs during the optimal development period for learning social skills. While you will want your puppy to learn some basic obedience skills in the more formal training segment of the class, make sure he will also get the opportunity to learn from safe socialization experiences. These experiences should include interaction with other puppies, adult dogs, unique environmental stimuli, and a variety of people (usually the other owners in the class) in a controlled, supervised setting.

Unfortunately, not all puppy classes are created equal. Take the time to call around and interview several training facilities if you are fortunate enough to have access to multiple puppy classes in your area. Below is a list of questions to help you decide which class is the best fit for you and your puppy.

**Are puppies introduced to each other slowly and calmly when they start class?** This is particularly important with herding dog puppies, who need to learn self-control in exciting, motion-filled situations. If puppies are released all at once to rush at each other, all that motion can quickly overwhelm your puppy's ability to remain calm.

**Are puppies divided up for playtime by play style as well as size?** Ideally, the class you choose will have enough physical space and staff to provide for more than one playgroup if the personalities and play styles of the puppies in class require that type of division. You never want your puppy to practice being a bully or a nerd who won't take no for an answer. If he only plays with other puppies who will tolerate his play style, that is *exactly* what he will learn. Your puppy needs to learn how to give and take during play, so he should play with puppies who are physically and behaviorally able to do that with him.

**Are socially appropriate adult dogs in the playgroup as well?** This is probably the most important question of all for herding dog owners to ask about playgroups. One of the best ways for puppies to learn how to behave appropriately around other dogs is to have them interact with a socially appropriate adult dog who isn't impressed by puppy antics. Kindergartners don't teach other kindergartners how to behave without the supervision of an adult teacher, so why rely solely on puppies to teach one another how to behave without the supervision of an adult dog?

**Are other owners involved in playtime to provide positive human socialization experiences for the puppies?** It is important for your puppy to meet as many people as possible, especially during the first four or five months of his life. Herding dog puppies tend to become aloof or even outright wary of strangers as they mature, so having plenty of experiences with strangers is vital to your puppy's behavioral development. Your puppy doesn't need to seek out attention from strangers, but he should be confident enough to tolerate attention when it is given to him.

**Are children allowed to interact with the puppies during playtime?** Again, it is important that your puppy meets young children, but you should be prepared to help both your puppy and the children maintain self-control. Do not allow your puppy to try to herd or control any child. You never want him to chase and possibly nip anyone, even in play. Children should also be taught how to play safely and calmly with puppies. If children are running freely in playgroup, it is far better to err on the side of caution and not put your puppy in the group than to risk him getting excited and nipping a child. Every interaction your puppy has with *anyone* or *anything* is a learning experience for him, so be sure he is learning what *you* want him to learn!

**Can I observe a class without my puppy?** Any reputable trainer should allow you to observe a class without your puppy, provided you simply watch and don't attempt to participate or ask questions about your puppy during class. Watch the dynamics between puppies, between puppies and owners, and between puppies, owners, and the instructor. Check out the physical layout of the class, how skirmishes are handled, and the teaching methods used in class. Does the instructor keep all the puppies safe during play? Is there a general atmosphere of respect in the class? How does your gut feel about the class? If you are uneasy about bringing your puppy to a particular class, listen to your gut, even if you can't readily identify why you aren't comfortable. If you are uneasy, your puppy will sense that and become uneasy as well.

You may feel uncomfortable calling a trainer and asking all these questions, but the impact early puppy classes can have over your herding dog's lifetime is tremendous. It is crucial you pick the best class you can for him. A reputable trainer will welcome questions about his class and will appreciate the effort you put into finding the best training situation possible for your puppy. Professional organizations such as the Association of Professional Dog Trainers, the National Association of Dog Obedience Instructors, and the Certification Council for Professional Dog Trainers can help you locate trainers most likely to offer appropriate classes for you and your puppy; see the Resources section at the end of this book for more information on these organizations.

### What if I don't have a choice in puppy classes?

If you don't have multiple options when it comes to early puppy classes for your herding dog, interview the instructor of the only class anyway. Then decide, based on the answers you receive, if that class will be a good fit for you and your puppy. If you have concerns, find out if the class can be adapted to fit your puppy's needs. Ultimately, only you can decide if the risk of your puppy learning bad habits in an early puppy class outweighs the benefits of participating in that class. Do not use lack of access to a suitable class as an excuse to avoid socializing your puppy. If you don't feel comfortable with the only early puppy class available to you, or if you live in an area where there aren't any early puppy classes available, you still need to work on your own as best you can to socialize your puppy if you want an adult dog who is confident and socially appropriate around other dogs. It may require more work on your part, but you can take your puppy around town to expose him to new environmental stimuli and, if you have access to friends with puppies or, more importantly, well-socialized adult dogs, you can make your own puppy playdates for socialization experiences. Your puppy can learn everything he needs to learn about proper canine communication from adult dogs who have good social skills. The adult dog should tolerate some play from the puppy (although he probably won't want to play as much as another puppy would) and if the puppy needs to be corrected, he should give a correction and then stop as soon as the puppy alters his behavior appropriately. If you don't have access to socially appropriate adult dogs or aren't sure if the dogs you are considering are actually appropriate, consult with a puppy class instructor. He should be able to help you find a good socialization partner for your puppy. Give your puppy as broad a range of experiences as possible so he learns to read dogs of different sizes, shapes, and personalities. There are many excellent books, training videos, and online training classes available to help you start to teach your young puppy basic manners; several of these training resources are listed in the Resources section at the end of this book.

## Older puppy and adult class selection

Dogs mentally and physically mature at different rates. Larger breed puppies, including most herding breeds, start showing adult social behaviors around six months, when their hormones begin kicking in and they enter their "teenager" phase. Play behaviors change significantly or begin to disappear altogether, sexual behaviors begin to increase, and arousal may start to tip over into potentially serious altercations between puppies if not defused quickly and appropriately. Puppies that played together wonderfully when they were three months old may start to show less tolerance for one another's antics as they mature. The need for continuous play with other dogs is no longer there; the critical brain development window for socialization has already closed. At this age, playing becomes more about learning self-control and tolerance around other dogs rather than chewing on and chasing every other dog around. Your teenage puppy should start to focus more on you than on other puppies and dogs.

If dogs are allowed to play with each other in a training class designed for adolescent or adult dogs, ask the instructor what purpose that interaction serves. Teaching your dog to maintain self-control and to pay attention to you when in close proximity to other dogs are appropriate reasons to allow brief, controlled, on-leash interactions between adult dogs in class. However, if the instructor tells you these encounters are supposed to teach your dog to play appropriately with other dogs, run, don't walk, away from that class. That is a potentially dangerous situation for your dog. The window to learn how to play appropriately with other dogs closes at about sixteen weeks of age. Dogs really only learn, at best, how to tolerate other dogs after that point in their lives. Even if your adult dog is socially appropriate, if your instructor wants to teach adult dogs to play with each other, it is a safe bet that at least one of your dog's classmates has a social deficit; being inappropriately friendly is just as problematic as being outright aggressive. Your herding dog may feel the need to control or correct that type of behavior, possibly leading to a serious altercation. Playtime between adult dogs should be done in a casual setting, between dogs who are known to enjoy interacting with other adult dogs. Adult playtime in class is risky and can cause serious behavioral harm if not carefully set up and managed.

Any training class should provide quality instruction based on humane, scientifically proven training methods. Your instructor should be able to adapt his training approach to meet the unique needs of you and your dog. Professional organizations and referrals from other herding dog owners are good places to start for locating a class for your teenage or adult herding dog. Before enrolling, ask if you can observe a class without your dog to help you decide if the class will be a good fit.

## What if my herding dog was already an adult when I got him?

If you choose to adopt an adult herding dog, it is important to understand that you may never be able to completely make up for any socialization deficits your dog already has. While an adult dog who was not properly socialized as a puppy can learn to tolerate the presence of other dogs and exhibit self-control, he may never be able to appropriately interact one-on-one with other dogs because of his lack of experience as a puppy. Alternatively, if he had negative experiences with other dogs at some time before you adopted him, he could react negatively to other dogs. You can teach him coping skills to help him with these weak areas, but it may require the assistance of a professional behaviorist and considerable time and effort on your part to achieve lasting behavioral changes. Do not overwhelm him or expect him to know better than to behave the way he is behaving; it will take time and effort for him to learn the new behaviors you expect of him. You must be willing to accept that an adult herding dog who did not learn appropriate canine communication skills as a puppy may never be willing or able to play appropriately with other dogs. And that's okay! Teach him to tolerate the presence of other appropriate dogs in his vicinity, but never try to force him to play with another dog. Chances are your dog won't end up learning anything positive from such an experience. Your adult herding dog may be perfectly content to hang out and work with you. And for most rescue dogs, simply having that human attention is a life-altering gift!

## A few words about dog parks and doggie daycare

Dog parks and doggie daycare facilities have become increasingly popular with urban dog owners. On the surface, dog parks and daycare seem like the perfect solution to exercising and socializing dogs, and indeed they are, for some dogs. Most dogs come home happy and exhausted after spending time in either place. However, before deciding to use a dog park or dog daycare to exercise your herding dog, it is important to understand the risks associated with taking your dog to either place and to know how to decide if your dog is truly playing or if there are more dangerous herding or pack interactions going on. Remember, proper social skills can only be learned from interacting with other dogs who already possess proper social skills while your dog is still a young puppy. Is your herding dog really learning how to behave appropriately around people and dogs when he is at the dog park or daycare running around with other dogs who possess unknown levels of social skills?

Any time two or more dogs are put together, a pack dynamic is created. Dogs in a pack may engage in behaviors that no individual member of the pack would do on his own. This dynamic can quickly become very dangerous. When you take your herding dog to the dog park or put him in daycare, you have little or no control over the other dogs he will meet. This can be just as problematic for adult dogs as it is for puppies. Play should always involve give and take between *all* the participants; a dog being chased should also have the chance to chase others. Unfortunately, when unacquainted dogs are put together to "play," many times one or two dogs end up being singled out and chased mercilessly by the rest of the impromptu pack that forms. This is more of a hunting activity than a play activity for all involved. All the dogs certainly go home tired, but for different reasons. The dogs who were being chased are just as exhausted from the mental stress of not being able to escape as from the physical exercise; the dogs who were chasing are exhausted from the physical exercise and the arousal that chasing causes. However, none of the dogs were actually "playing" and they have all learned undesirable social lessons. There is a very fine line between this type of interaction and actual predation. The dogs who couldn't escape learn to fear other dogs, and the dogs who chased learn to be canine bullies.

*Although both dogs were tired after this interaction, Shishka was not playing appropriately with Ember. She was practicing inappropriate herding behaviors on a puppy who could not tell her to stop. Fortunately she was interrupted and redirected away from Ember shortly after this photograph was taken.*

Chase games are particularly problematic for herding dogs. Your dog's instinct to control motion, coupled with his tenacity and focus, can make him act like a relentless dog park or daycare bully. He may spend his time at the dog park constantly trying to micromanage every move the other dogs make. As long as his efforts to control the other dogs are successful, he will continue to try to control any dog who comes into the park. But eventually, he is going to meet a dog who won't respond to that control, and your dog may become frustrated. The situation can quickly escalate and your dog may resort to physical contact in an effort to regain control of the other dog. This sets the stage for a fight. Just because your herding dog is in constant motion at the dog park, do not assume it is safe or appropriate for him to be there.

Some dog owners, in particular those who think of their dogs as human child substitutes, have a hard time accepting that most adult dogs don't need or want to play with other dogs in the same way they wanted to play when they were puppies. Puppies play to practice the skills they would need to survive if they were in the wild. They stalk, chase, grab, and nip at each other to perfect the crucial pieces of the predatory behavior chain. They also learn to "speak dog" to one another and interact appropriately with other dogs. Puppies undoubtedly enjoy playing with each other, but the primary purpose behind play is to learn survival and social skills. As puppies mature, the need for this type of interaction with other dogs naturally diminishes as the lessons are presumably learned. Dogs who have been bred to work alone (like most terrier breeds) often lose the desire to play with other dogs far sooner than do those dogs who have been bred to work more closely with other dogs and people (like retrievers). When socially appropriate adult dogs who know each other get together, they are more likely to engage in casual environmental exploration and just hang out together rather than wrestling, chasing, and chewing on each other like puppies. This is perfectly normal; no amount of exposure to other dogs is going to change that.

While it is true that many people take their herding dogs to dog parks and daycares every day and never have any problems, the chances are still extremely high that someday the circumstances will be just right and your dog will have a negative experience. Are you willing to take that chance with him? Be sure you don't try to impose *your* desire for your dog to have canine playmates on your dog by taking him to the dog park. Similarly, if you put your dog in daycare, be sure you are doing it for *his* benefit, rather than as a means to assuage your guilt for leaving him during the workday or not taking time to exercise him yourself. There are legitimate benefits for some dogs in some circumstances to go to dog parks and daycares, but those benefits don't apply to every dog. Weigh the actual quality of life your dog would have without dog parks and daycare (from *his* point of view, not yours) against the risk that he will learn bad habits or get hurt, before you decide to put him in either situation. Many behavioral problems that owners try to solve through dog parks and daycare can be altered more effectively simply by providing their dogs more structured exercise at home and spending time actually teaching them how to behave. If you spend fifteen minutes driving to the dog park, thirty minutes allowing your dog to run there, and another fifteen minutes driving back home, you already have access to one hour in your daily schedule in which you can provide your dog meaningful exercise with you and plenty of training to keep his mind healthy and to teach him exactly how you would like him to behave. That may be a better way to spend your time with your dog, particularly from your dog's point of view, than forcing him into a group of unknown dogs to "play."

# Chapter 5

## How Do Dogs Learn?

---

*The dog calls forth, on the one hand, the best that a human person is capable of;*
*self-sacrificing devotion to a weaker and dependent being and, on the other hand, the*
*temptation to exercise power in a willful and arbitrary, even perverse, manner.*
*Both traits can exist in the same person.*

*Yi-Fu Tuan*
*Dominance & Affection: The Making of Pets*

Urban life with a herding dog can be exceptionally challenging if you do not provide adequate physical and mental activities for him on a daily basis. Instinctive herding dog behaviors are often in direct contradiction with the behaviors you want in your pet, and you may find yourself spending tremendous amounts of time and energy trying to teach your herding dog to stop acting like the very dog he is. The goal of dog training should never be to make your dog into a furry, four-legged human or to force him to submit to your every whim and fancy. The goal of dog training should be to help him learn how to behave appropriately as a canine family member, while still allowing him to be the wonderful, unique dog he is. Dogs don't think the way humans do; they don't have the same problem-solving abilities, the same sense of "right" and "wrong," or even the same perception of time that people do. To effectively and humanely train any dog, you need to understand how dogs learn. Then you need to use that knowledge so training will be enjoyable for the living beings on both ends of the leash. A basic overview of canine learning theory will help you get started.

## Learning theory overview

Learning theory is a vast, fascinating field of study. There are many books that delve into the myriad details about how animals learn, such as Pamela Reid's *Excel-erated Learning*, listed in the Resources section at the end of this book. This chapter will explain just a few basic learning theory concepts and terms to help you learn how to train your dog in a way that makes sense to him, so he will be able to learn what you want *him* to learn more quickly and easily.

## Classical conditioning

Dogs learn in several different ways. Two of these are particularly relevant to most training you will do with your herding dog. One way is **classical conditioning**. This is the type of learning Ivan Pavlov saw in his research dogs (sometimes referred to as "Pavlovian learning"). Pavlov studied digestive physiology in dogs. All healthy dogs begin to drool to some extent when they see and smell food. This is not a behavior they learn to do consciously; it is a subconscious, automatic physiological response by their bodies to get ready to consume food. However, Pavlov noticed his research dogs also began to drool at the sight of the kennel assistant who was in charge of feeding them, even when there was not any food around. Based on this observation, Pavlov predicted that if he put something in the dogs' environment immediately before the dogs were given food, they would eventually associate that new stimulus with food, too. Given enough repetitions, the dogs would start to drool at the presence of that stimulus, in anticipation of the food to follow, even when no food was actually present. His most famous way of testing his hypothesis was by ringing a bell immediately prior to giving the dogs food. At first, the dogs didn't drool at the sound of the bell alone; they didn't associate that sound with food. But once that association was made through consistently ringing the bell immediately before giving the dogs food, the dogs began drooling at the sound of the bell, the same way they drooled at the sight and smell of food. The sound of the bell became what is known as a **conditioned reinforcer**. The bell became associated with the delivery of food and the dogs responded by drooling, just the same as they responded to food, because they knew, based on experience, food was on its way. This is the same mode of learning at play when a dog learns to associate the sound of a clicker with the delivery of something he wants. By repeatedly pairing the sound of a clicker with the delivery of a treat, the dog subconsciously begins to associate the unique clicking sound with getting a reward.

## Operant conditioning

**Operant conditioning** is the other common mode of learning that is particularly relevant to dog training. This type of learning happens when a dog makes an association between his conscious behavior and the consequence that immediately follows that behavior. If the consequence that immediately follows the behavior is something the dog likes, the behavior is more likely to happen again. If the consequence that immediately follows the behavior is something he doesn't like, the behavior is not as likely to happen again. By controlling the consequences that follow a dog's behavior, you can affect the likelihood that the behavior will be repeated. If you have heard the term "positive reinforcement training," you have heard of one quadrant of operant conditioning.

Operant conditioning is divided into four quadrants, or variations, based on the way consequences are manipulated immediately following a behavior. The four quadrants are positive reinforcement, negative reinforcement, positive punishment, and negative punishment. In operant conditioning, the terms **positive** and **negative** simply mean *adding* (positive) or *subtracting* (negative) something from your dog's environment to influence the likelihood your dog will perform a particular behavior again. **Reinforcement** is anything that *increases* the likelihood a behavior will occur again, while **punishment** is anything that *decreases* the likelihood a behavior will occur again. Training sometimes involves crossing quadrants, so it is useful to have a basic understanding of what all four quadrants are and how they work.

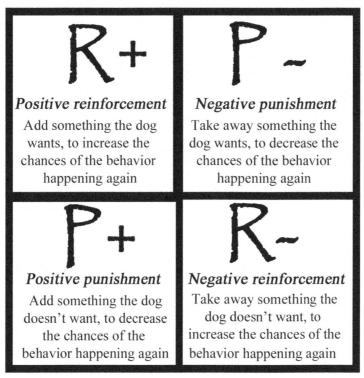

| R+ | P~ |
|---|---|
| *Positive reinforcement*<br>Add something the dog wants, to increase the chances of the behavior happening again | *Negative punishment*<br>Take away something the dog wants, to decrease the chances of the behavior happening again |
| P+ | R~ |
| *Positive punishment*<br>Add something the dog doesn't want, to decrease the chances of the behavior happening again | *Negative reinforcement*<br>Take away something the dog doesn't want, to increase the chances of the behavior happening again |

*Understanding how operant conditioning works will help make your training more effective.*

**Positive reinforcement** involves immediately adding something your dog wants to his environment when he performs a desired behavior. By reinforcing your dog for a desired behavior, you increase the likelihood that the behavior will continue to occur in the future. For example, if you say "Sit" and your dog sits, you might give him a treat he likes as a reinforcer for that behavior. The dog performed a desired behavior and you "added" a treat to his environment as a consequence of that behavior—you have used positive reinforcement to increase the likelihood that the next time you say "Sit," your dog will sit in order to obtain another treat. Most people are familiar with this quadrant of operant conditioning.

**Positive punishment** involves immediately adding something the dog wants to avoid to his environment when the dog performs an undesired behavior. This quadrant decreases the likelihood the behavior will occur in the future. The dog will change his behavior to avoid the unpleasant addition to his environment. For example, if you say "Sit" and your dog stands there and stares at you instead of sitting, you give him a sharp slap on the rump to get him to sit. By adding a punisher to your dog's environment when he performs an incorrect behavior (a slap on the rump for standing instead of sitting), you decrease the chances that your dog will stand the next time you say "Sit." Your dog performs the correct, or at least a different, behavior to avoid something he finds unpleasant when you train using positive punishment. Unfortunately, while he may sit the next time to avoid a slap, he may also shake with fear as he does it, depending on his response to the punisher.

**Negative punishment** involves immediately subtracting something the dog wants from his environment when the dog performs an undesired behavior. This quadrant also decreases the likelihood the behavior will occur again in the future. For instance, if you cue your dog to sit so a person can approach and pet him, but instead of promptly sitting, he starts trying to jump up on the approaching person, you ask the person to immediately turn and walk away from your dog. You are using negative punishment to decrease the likelihood that the next time you say "Sit," your dog will jump up instead, because you took what the dog wants (attention from the approaching person) away when the dog performed an undesired behavior (jumping up). Most of us tend to think of punishment only as some type of unpleasant physical contact. But punishers can also involve the loss of opportunity to obtain something desirable. Losing the chance to be petted can be an effective punishment for a dog that really enjoys interacting with people. For many herding dogs, losing the chance to perform another behavior (i.e., to keep working with you) can also be a powerful punisher.

**Negative reinforcement** involves immediately subtracting something the dog wants to avoid from his environment when he performs a correct behavior. This quadrant increases the likelihood the behavior will occur in the future. Using this quadrant of operant conditioning, when you say "Sit," you might also immediately give a sharp collar correction upward, putting unpleasant pressure on your dog's neck. As soon as your dog's rear hits the floor, you release the pressure. You removed something the dog wanted to avoid (pressure on his neck) when the dog performed the desired behavior (sit), thereby increasing the likelihood that your dog will sit the next time you say "Sit." This quadrant is more prevalent in traditional training methods, such as the pinched-ear method of teaching a dog to retrieve an object.

## Which quadrants work best with a herding dog?

If you understand the basics of operant conditioning, you understand why various training techniques work and how to train your dog fairly and effectively. Although all four quadrants of learning theory will work to increase desired behaviors and decrease undesired behaviors, using positive reinforcement and negative punishment works best the vast majority of the time. Historically, many trainers who worked with dogs actually used for herding relied heavily on positive punishment. Fortunately, many trainers now understand operant conditioning better and rely more on positive reinforcement to train working herding dogs. By giving your dog something he wants in exchange for performing a behavior that you want, and withholding what he wants when he doesn't, you will establish a fair, respectful working relationship that you can readily manipulate to bring out the best in your dog. In addition to being learner-friendly and humane quadrants to work in, positive reinforcement and negative punishment are less likely to trigger adverse behavioral responses from dogs than are negative reinforcement and positive punishment.

A brief note concerning terminology: the terms **reward** and **correction** are often used in everyday dog training discussions to describe the consequences given to a dog as a result of his behavior, instead of the scientifically correct terms "reinforcer" and "punisher." To avoid confusion, the more common terms "reward" and "correction" will be used for the remainder of this book to mean the same thing as "reinforcer" and "punisher."

## The four stages of learning

Regardless of which quadrant of operant conditioning is used to teach a new behavior, learning is rarely an instantaneous event. Most learning occurs in stages, over time, and not in a completely constant progression of improvement. It is important to understand these four learning stages so you can maintain the behaviors you taught your dog in training class long after the class has ended. Training classes may get your dog through the first stage of learning, but you will need to keep working with him after the class ends to get through the rest of the stages; and you will need to go through this process for every behavior you teach him.

The first stage in learning any new behavior involves acquiring new knowledge. This is the step most people think of when they think about "learning" or "training." The second stage involves using that new knowledge until the learner is fluent, or automatic, in its use. The third stage involves applying this new knowledge to other situations where it is relevant. The fourth stage involves maintaining the knowledge for the learner's lifetime so that the knowledge becomes part of the learner's behavioral repertoire.

Let's look at how the four stages of learning apply to teaching your dog how to sit on cue. When you first start teaching your dog to sit, he has no idea what you expect him to do when you say "Sit." He must learn how to lift his head up and back, shift his weight back, lower his rump all the way to the floor, tuck his feet underneath himself, and move his tail into a comfortable position, all just to perform the simple behavior you call "Sit." Initially, you will have to help him figure out how to accomplish all this. It takes a lot of mental concentration for your dog to focus on what you want and move all his body parts correctly. He is acquiring new knowledge in the first stage of the learning process.

Eventually, with enough repetitions and experience, your dog starts sitting on his own when you say the word "Sit." His actions become automatic when you say that word, and he can begin to perform this behavior reliably in familiar places with few distractions around. You don't have to help him into a sit now; he knows how to move his body into position. He is in the second stage of learning and is becoming fluent in performing a sit behavior. He no longer has to concentrate as much to physically sit on cue.

As your dog obtains even more experience with "Sit," you start cueing him to perform that behavior in different places or around different distractions. You ask for the behavior outside in the yard, in the park, or while someone comes through your front door. You are broadening your dog's experience with "Sit" and asking him to perform that behavior in many different situations. This is the third stage in the learning process, where your dog learns that "Sit" means sit, no matter where he is or what is going on around him. Bob Bailey, a world-renowned animal trainer with decades of experience training many different species, points out that when you teach an animal a new behavior, you spend approximately 10% of your time actually teaching the behavior and 90% of your time developing the animal's environmental confidence so he learns to perform the behavior anytime, anyplace. In competitive obedience training, this is referred to as "proofing" the behavior.

This third stage is often the one that dog owners skip over during their training. Yet it really should be the one that is given the most time and effort. Dogs do not generalize new learned behaviors to different situations very well; they have to be shown that "Sit" means sit, whether you are in the living room, in the front yard, or at the park. Learning to sit in one environment doesn't automatically mean your dog will understand how to sit in a different one. This is why so many dogs will do beautiful sits at home but can't do a single sit when they come to class. The dogs have not generalized the sit behavior to locations outside their homes yet.

Integrating the sit behavior into your dog's everyday life so he maintains that behavior is the fourth stage of learning. If you cue your dog to sit as a regular part of his lifestyle, he will continue to perform that behavior for the rest of his life. If, however, you quit asking for the behavior as soon as your training class ends, it will soon weaken and your dog will eventually begin to perform it less reliably. It isn't enough to spend a few weeks out of your dog's life teaching him to sit in training class; you have to incorporate this behavior into your herding dog's everyday life to keep it strong. The more difficult the behavior is for your dog to perform, the quicker it will deteriorate if you quit asking him to perform it on a regular basis.

## Embrace the mistakes

Learning does not happen in a straight line. When you first start teaching your dog a new behavior, you will probably see your dog perform with flashes of brilliance, combined with periods of averageness and occasional moments of total disaster. As your dog gains a better understanding of the new behavior, you will notice that his brilliant performances become more frequent and his mistakes become less frequent over time. The general learning trend moves toward "perfection," even though there have been some highs and lows in the training process. Ideally, your training plan will keep mistakes to a bare minimum so your dog's learning happens as smoothly and quickly as possible; but no matter how carefully you set up your training sessions, your dog *will* make a mistake now and then. There is no such thing as 100% consistent, perfect performance, for dogs or people. Mistakes are a normal part of the learning process.

Try not to get frustrated or give up when mistakes happen. Mistakes are nothing more than pieces of information that will allow you to assess what your dog does and does not understand at any particular point in the training process. If you look at mistakes as information to help you refine your training, you will continue to improve your dog's understanding of the behavior you are teaching him and avoid unproductive emotional responses that could harm your relationship with your dog. For example, if you are working on teaching your dog to sit and he performs brilliantly in your home but seems to forget that he has ever heard the cue "Sit" before when you are in your front yard, consider this "mistake" as information. Your dog is showing you he doesn't understand that he can and should sit on cue even when he is outside, or telling you that he isn't motivated enough to sit when he is in the yard. Use this information to set up future training sessions where you help your dog be successful in performing a sit on your front lawn. Eventually, your dog will only occasionally make mistakes when cued to sit, no matter where he is, and you will know how to keep him motivated to perform in many different situations. Embrace your dog's mistakes and use them in a positive way to help your dog learn what you are trying to teach him.

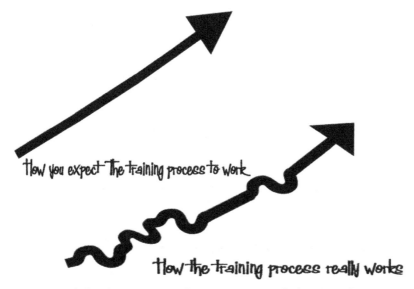

How you expect the training process to work

How the training process really works

*Keep in mind that learning never happens in a straight line. Use deviations in progress as information to create effective training sessions for your dog.*

## The 80% rule

Sometimes it is difficult to decide when to make the training more challenging for your dog, particularly as his fluency increases. One handy yardstick to use when deciding if your dog is ready for you to add more challenges to his training environment is the 80% rule. Cue your dog to perform whatever behavior you are working on five times in a training session. If your dog can perform the behavior (1) the *first* time, (2) with a *single* cue, (3) in the *manner you want* the behavior performed, (4) on *80%* of the repetitions (four out of five times) in a single training session, (5) over *three or four separate training sessions*, he is probably ready for you to make the training a little more difficult so his behavioral fluency will continue to improve. You might increase the duration of the behavior, the difficulty of the environmental distractions, or the distance between you and your dog while he is performing the behavior to continue building his fluency. Be honest! There is no prize for trying to force your dog to handle distractions that he isn't ready for yet. If you cheat in your behavioral analysis of your dog, you will slow down your training. It's okay if he can't do the behavior four out of five times when you test him. That information tells you he isn't ready for challenges that are more difficult yet. Keep working at his current level of difficulty until he is successful at least 80% of the time before increasing the difficulty again. If he can't perform even one successful repetition in a training session, that information tells you he needs a slightly less difficult environment to work in at this point in his learning, or he needs more motivation to perform the behavior in the first place. Make his environment less distracting and work awhile longer on the behavior until he is truly ready to handle challenges that are more difficult.

If 4 out of 5 times
Your dog responds
just fine,
You can change
something in your
training,
But only one thing at
a time!

*Keeping the 80% rule in mind will help you keep your dog's training moving forward effectively.*

# Knowing vs. doing

Training a dog always involves a certain amount of guesswork. You must rely on the imperfect method of observing your dog's outward behavior to guess whether or not learning has occurred, since you have no way to peek inside his skull and see the microscopic changes that occur in the brain as learning physically takes place. Nevertheless, if your dog performs the correct behavior on a single cue at least 80% of the time you cue him to perform it, you can reasonably infer he has learned to perform that behavior in that particular environment. But just because your dog knows how to perform a behavior doesn't necessarily mean he will always perform it on cue. You are dealing with a living, thinking, feeling, independent, complex being. You aren't 100% consistent in performing learned behaviors, so is it fair to expect your dog to be 100% consistent performing learned behaviors?

Many things affect whether your dog will perform a learned behavior. He may not be feeling well, something in the environment may be literally interfering with his ability to perform the behavior, or he may not understand that he can perform the behavior in a specific environment. Stress may be affecting his performance. You may be confusing him by not giving clear, consistent cues. He also might not perform a learned behavior simply because he is not motivated enough to perform at that particular moment. Motivation reflects what is most important to a dog at any given point in time and the amount of effort he is willing to put into gaining what is important to him. Lack of motivation does not mean a dog chooses to avoid performing a behavior just to get even with you for something that happened earlier in the day or because he wants to make you mad. It simply means that, from your dog's point of view, there isn't enough value in gaining the reward or avoiding the correction for him to perform the learned behavior you cued him to perform. He may know how to perform the behavior but still not do it because he is not sufficiently motivated. Learning how to motivate your dog effectively will help you help your dog perform learned behaviors more consistently. Chapter 6 is devoted completely to coaching you through how to do just that. Learning to make educated guesses about the reasons your dog doesn't perform a behavior you assume he has learned will help you make more effective training choices and greatly enhance his performance consistency.

# Say what you mean; mean what you say

Inconsistent use of cues is another reason your dog might not perform a behavior consistently. Dogs don't understand human language the way people do. Consider the phrase "Sit down." If you tell a person to sit down, he will probably understand you want him to assume a seated position. But if your dog already understands the behaviors you want when you say "Sit" and "Down" separately, he may respond very differently if you cue him to "Sit down." He *should* understand your phrase "Sit down" as a two-link behavior chain; first a sit, followed immediately by a down. Therefore, the correct way for your dog to respond is to sit, then lie down. If you actually wanted him to sit when you said "Sit down," you might think your dog didn't do what you told him to do because he ended up lying down. Yet, in reality, your dog did *exactly* what you told him to do. He responded to your literal verbal cue, instead of your implied meaning.

Another possible response from your dog when you say "Sit down" is to simply sit. You probably would not think of this as an incorrect response to your cue "Sit down," because you know you actually *intended* for him to sit. Nevertheless, you *told* him to sit and then lie down. If your dog didn't lie down, it means that either your dog doesn't actually understand the down cue yet or, for some reason, he didn't perform the down behavior. Either way, if you don't help your dog lie down, he is learning he doesn't always need to lie down when you cue him to "Down." A third possible response from your dog may be that he lies down without sitting first; this is also incorrect based on the words you used to cue him.

Words have very specific meanings to your dog, so you need to be sure you use your training words carefully and consistently to help your dog perform behaviors reliably. Say exactly what you mean, and mean exactly what you say. If you want him to sit, tell him "Sit," instead of "Sit down." If you follow that rule, your dog will have an easier time doing what you want him to do. Pick a unique, distinct cue for each behavior you teach him and then use that cue consistently. For example, don't use the cue "Down" to mean lie down in some situations and get off the sofa or stop jumping on you in other situations. The specific words you use don't really matter; you can teach your dog to come to you when he hears the word "Jeep" and to sit when he hears the word "Mustang" if you want. As long as you teach your dog the exact behavior you expect when you say a particular word, and consistently use that word to cue that one behavior only, your dog will understand what you expect him to do. The same rule applies to physical cues; use one discrete motion for each discrete behavior you want to be able to cue with physical signals. If you point your finger to the floor to cue your dog to sit, use a different motion to cue him to lie down. Be as consistent as possible with your physical cues to help your dog distinguish them from all the other motions you do throughout the day.

## What they learn first, they learn best

Think about how you want to interact with your herding dog after he has learned what you expect of him. Do you want to be forced to raise your voice and move like a bad break-dancer to get your dog's attention and response? Or do you want to be able to give your dog cues in a normal, conversational tone of voice and use calm, clear, and simple physical cues when necessary? There is a huge difference between being enthusiastic and being crazy in how you train and reward your dog. There certainly are times when whooping and hollering in excitement could be appropriate to let your dog know just how awesome he is, but most of the time, a calm, sincere show of affection, verbal praise, or other appropriate reward is the best fit with the business-like attitude of the typical herding dog. If you start working with your dog in the manner you would like to work with him for his lifetime, he will never know any other way to interact with you. If you raise your voice and jump around when you are first teaching him a behavior, he will eventually expect that type of behavior from you every time the two of you interact.

In moments of stress, behavior deteriorates. Stress can be created by things the dog wants to have or things the dog wants to avoid. Excitement and fear are both forms of stress and can interfere with your dog's performance. Under sufficient stress, learned behaviors can deteriorate to the performance level when first learned. What does this mean for dog training? If you had to yell, jump around, and wave cookies to get your dog's attention when you first taught him to pay attention to you, then you may have to resort to those extremes to get his attention when he is under significant stress, because his attention behavior deteriorated to its earlier performance level, when all that effort by you was necessary to get his attention. Start teaching any behavior in a calm, conversational tone, with confidence, enthusiasm, sincerity, and the minimum amount of extra body language possible. This will increase the odds you will not have to resort to histrionics or excess physical effort to get your dog to perform the same behavior when he is stressed.

## Teach, then label

As mentioned earlier, learning does not occur in a straight line. Even the best dog trainer in the world can rarely get the final desired behavior from a dog the first time, every time, when the dog is learning a new behavior. Experimentation and mistakes happen on both ends of the leash. Your dog doesn't know what you expect him to do when you first start teaching him a new behavior, and you may not know exactly how to communicate to him what you want him to do. He probably won't perform the behavior as quickly or perfectly as you want the first few times he does it. If you start putting a verbal cue with a behavior when you first start teaching it, all those imperfections will be included in your dog's understanding of what he needs to do when he hears that cue. However, if you wait to add in your cue word until you have a very close approximation of the final behavior you want from your dog, his understanding of that cue will only include the near-perfect performance of the behavior you are teaching him. For example, when you teach your dog to lie down, he may move slowly into position the first few repetitions, trying to figure out what you want him to do. You may be kneeling or sitting on the ground next to him, luring him into position. He may try to resist lying down and actually stand up at some point. He might lie down very slowly until he starts to gain understanding and fluency. Alternatively, he may drop his front end down and leave his back end sticking up in the air. If you say "Down" and then try to get him to lie down, all that extra behavioral "junk" may become associated with the cue. He may think a slow, leisurely stretch into a down is what you want when you say "Down." When your dog is under stress, he may revert to performing the down behavior the way he first performed it on cue, which would include all the mistakes and slow responses naturally involved in the learning process.

Waiting until your dog is fluent with the down behavior before associating the final verbal or physical cue with its performance will keep the behavior cleaner and less prone to excessive deterioration under stress. If you delay putting a verbal cue to the down behavior until he is consistently lying down quickly and completely, your dog's behavioral association with the verbal cue "Down" will only include quick, complete drops.

## Management vs. training

Management involves manipulating your dog's environment to increase or decrease the opportunity your dog has to perform a particular behavior; training involves manipulating the consequences that follow your dog's behavior to increase or decrease the likelihood that he will continue to perform that behavior in the future. Management can provide a quick fix for many unacceptable behaviors your dog already performs, so you can retain your sanity while working through the slower process of training new, acceptable behaviors. Management can also prevent unacceptable behaviors from being learned in the first place. Your dog won't learn how to behave appropriately by management alone, but you can often get immediate behavioral results that will help the learning process if you combine management techniques with training.

Let's say you have a dog who, for several years, has been allowed to jump on anyone who walks through your door. Now you decide to teach him to sit politely when guests come into your home. To achieve this, you must train your dog to sit, to stay in that position until released, and to ignore people coming into your home. This learning will take time! And during that time, guests will continue to come to your home. If your dog is allowed to jump on guests between training sessions, it will be more difficult to teach him to stop jumping and sit still for guests. To speed up the learning process and minimize confusion, you should train the new door greeting behaviors while simultaneously using environmental management to prevent him from jumping on guests when you are not with the dog. There are many different ways to manage your dog's environment to stop him from jumping. Putting him on a leash *before* your guests come in, so you can keep him near you, or putting him in another room when guests arrive, so he doesn't even have access to those people until he has calmed down, are just two options to manage his door greeting behavior. Through management, you are removing the opportunity for him to continue to do what you no longer want him to do. If you prevent your dog from carrying out an unacceptable behavior while you are also teaching him an acceptable one to perform in its place, you will change his behavior more quickly and minimize frustration for both of you.

Environmental management is also an easy way to keep dogs from learning bad habits in the first place. If shoes are put away where your dog can't get to them, he can never learn that chewing on them is fun. If he is never allowed to jump on guests, he won't do it to get attention. Having your dog drag a long line when running in the yard will keep him from playing "catch me if you can" when you want him to come in. Managing your dog's environment so that he is only able to do what you want him to do is, in theory, a relatively easy way to curb bad behaviors in your dog. Of course, reality makes that much environmental management unrealistic. People forget to put their shoes in the closet, guests may encourage your dog to jump up on them, or your dog may sneak out the door without a long line on. In spite of your best intentions, your dog may develop bad habits. But if you develop a good training plan and combine that with the most consistent environmental management possible in your home, you can nip bad habits in the bud and help your herding dog behave in ways that make him a true joy to have as part of the family.

## Know when to say when

Sometimes the most difficult part of training any dog is knowing when to stop a training session early. For many different reasons, a training session may fall apart. Your dog may be frustrated. You may have a splitting headache. Your dog may have a touch of arthritis that is causing him discomfort. You may be struggling to clear your mind of the problems you dealt with at work. Your spouse or children may be uncooperative in giving you a few minutes alone with your dog to train. You may have to go out of town on business. These situations happen to everyone; they are all part of that thing called "life." Sometimes when life happens and you or your dog isn't able to fully engage in your training session, it is more productive in the long run to call it a day and try again later than to try to bully your way through a session and risk creating more problems than you fix. If you find yourself losing patience with your dog, stop the session and try again when you are more composed and focused. If either of you is in significant physical pain, address the pain before trying to address the training. Herding dogs do not tolerate being frustrated or being unable to perform behaviors due to physical limitations. There is no harm in ending a training session early when the potential costs of continuing outweigh the possible benefits; the harm comes when your training deviation becomes a habit and you quit training entirely. Training is a lifelong project. Cutting an occasional training session short, or missing one entirely because of life, is sometimes the best training you can do!

# Chapter 6

## Becoming More Valuable Than Livestock in the Eyes of Your Herding Dog

*The dog's agenda is simple, fathomable, overt: I want. "I want to go out, come in, eat something, lie here, play with that, kiss you." There are no ulterior motives with a dog, no mind games, no second-guessing, no complicated negotiations or bargains, and no guilt trips or grudges if a request is denied.*

*Caroline Knapp*
*American author*

Knowing how to motivate your dog to bring out the best in him is critical to training success. It is unrealistic to expect your dog to do what you ask him to do simply because you ask him to do it. Even though it is a rather romantic fiction that a dog should work simply to please his owner, the truth is, no dog works simply because he is told to do so, not even a workaholic herding dog. Your dog needs to gain something he wants or needs from working with you. What he gains may be your attention, a treat, the opportunity to do something else he likes to do, or the ability to avoid something he doesn't like, but he needs to gain *something* when he does what you ask him to do or he won't do it in the first place. Motivating your dog is all about figuring out what he wants or needs, and then using those things to enhance your dog's performance.

Every time you work with your dog, you are competing for his attention against all the other things in his environment. You will rarely be the most exciting thing around; there will usually be things that your dog finds far more interesting or exciting than you, particularly when you are outside. You will never move the same way as a squirrel or sheep would move, no matter how crazy you act. You will never sound like a squeaky toy or another dog barking, even if you scream nutty baby talk at the top of your lungs. You will never be chewy like a tennis ball. And 99.999% of the time, you will not smell as inviting as a dead, rotting animal carcass will. So to expect to be the most interesting or exciting thing in your dog's life all of the time is not realistic. Squirrels, sheep, toys, other dogs, balls, and stinking dead animals are all potentially far more exciting and interesting to your herding dog than you can ever be. But fortunately, to train your dog effectively, you do not have to be more exciting than other things competing for his attention; you only need to be more valuable to him. You can become more valuable than everything else simply by controlling your dog's access to all those other interesting, exciting things. Becoming the gatekeeper for access to whatever your dog is willing to work for makes you more valuable than any of those other things and helps you motivate your dog to do whatever you ask, in exchange for the access he wants to more exciting things. Building this value requires careful attention to reward selection, consistent and fair use of rewards, and patience. You must prove to your dog that when he looks to you for direction and does what you tell him to do, you will give him access to something that is worth the effort he made for you. There is so much more to motivating any dog than simply throwing a treat at him or patting him on the head. Building up a collection of verbal, physical, and environmental rewards that are very motivating to your herding dog will help you become that respected, valuable gatekeeper who is almost always able to motivate him to work with you, regardless of all the other distractions around. The rest of this chapter will help you create a collection of rewards that will greatly enhance your value in the eyes of your herding dog.

## Who determines what can be used as a reward?

In order to become more valuable than livestock in your herding dog's eyes, you have to identify rewards that will motivate your dog to work with you. Who determines what these rewards are? Your dog, of course! It doesn't matter how interesting you think a toy is or how well a certain type of treat has worked as a reward for someone else's dog. If *your* dog is not motivated enough to work for that particular treat or toy, it won't be an effective reward. Similarly, your dog also determines what constitutes a correction. If you frown at your dog and he rolls on his back and submissively urinates, you know that your body language is a powerful correction from his point of view, even if you didn't *intend* to correct him with your unhappy appearance. For many herding dogs, merely withholding the opportunity to continue working with you is a powerful correction. Training with your herding dog will go much more quickly and successfully if you remember your dog is the one in charge of identifying potential rewards and corrections.

## What can be used as a reward?

Nearly everything your dog wants in his life can be used as a reward. Most dog owners think of praise or treats when they think of rewards, but this is only the very tip of the reward iceberg. Think like your herding dog and all of a sudden, the world becomes one gigantic cookie jar filled with countless rewards for you to use! Watch what your dog chooses to pay attention to when he is left alone to do whatever he wants. Dogs don't lie about what interests them, so why waste time guessing at what your dog might be willing to work for, when he is showing you these things all the time? Almost anything that interests your dog can be used as a reward, as long as (1) the item is safe for both you and your dog, (2) your dog's access to it can be controlled during training, (3) it can promptly be delivered after a correct performance (or withheld after an incorrect performance), and (4) it is practical to use. With careful observation, you can start building an extensive collection of non-food rewards to use when training. You can even include "naughty" behaviors in your reward list—running, barking, and jumping can all be used as rewards, as long as *you* can start and end the behavior and your dog is only allowed to engage in the behavior *after* he has performed the behavior you asked him to do. If you try to prevent your dog from ever interacting with a distraction or engaging in "naughty" behaviors (i.e., those that are safe for him to do but that you find unacceptable), you will not necessarily decrease his desire for them. The longer he is denied any opportunity to engage in such behaviors, the stronger his desire may become to engage in them at all costs. Most of these naughty behaviors are simply normal dog behaviors that are unacceptable in modern human society. Giving your dog the chance just to be a dog is a powerful way to motivate your dog to do what you ask of him.

## Food

Most of us are familiar with using dog treats to train dogs. Food is a powerful intrinsic motivator; you do not typically have to encourage a healthy dog to eat. Every dog alive today is food-motivated to some extent, since he is obviously motivated to eat enough food to survive. With a little creativity and perseverance, you can find some type of food to use during training for even the most finicky eater. Treats are often the first type of reward used when teaching your dog a new behavior, because they can be given quickly and are relatively easy to use during training sessions.

Herding dogs can sometimes be difficult to motivate strictly with food. Their hard-driving desire to work sometimes overrides their immediate desire to eat and, if given a choice, many herding dogs would rather have a more physical reward for their efforts, such as retrieving a ball, playing tug, or even performing a different learned behavior, instead of a mere treat. But treats are very handy as rewards, particularly in training class and other situations where you don't have the time, space, or ability to use other types of rewards for your dog. Because herding dogs can be fussy about the types of treats they will eat when training, you should offer your dog highly valuable tidbits to encourage him to learn to work for treats. If he isn't interested in any other type of food, use a portion of his regular meals as treats and he can earn part of his meal while he is training.

Be creative when choosing training treats. For herding dogs who are not fussy about what they eat, you have a whole range of treat options available. Experiment with a selection of treats to see which ones really interest your dog. Instead of pre-packaged dog treats, try treats like skinless chicken, string cheese, homemade dog treats, dried apples, sweet potato chips, raw carrot slices, dehydrated beef heart, blueberry bagels, green tripe, dried squid, or anything else you can think of that is safe for him to eat. Never give your dog food containing chocolate, cocoa, raisins, onions, xylitol (an artificial sweetener commonly found in chewing gum), or high amounts of fat or salt. If your dog has severe food allergies, you can try to get his regular diet in an alternative form for use when training. For example, if you feed a special kibble diet, see if that same food is available in a canned version that you can let the dog lick off a spoon or from a food tube (available in most camping supply stores); alternatively, there are dog treat recipes available online that use ground kibble instead of flour that can be adapted to make special-diet training treats. If you have an exceptionally finicky eater who is not even interested in cooked chicken or beef with excess fat removed, low-fat cheese cubes, or water-packed tuna, you can use his regular kibble as a reward. Since your dog eats enough to stay alive, his regular food should work as a last-ditch food reward choice. Remember, no matter how tasty *you* might think a particular treat is or should be, it is your *dog* who is in charge of deciding which treats will work best as food rewards, and which treats will work in stressful situations.

In addition to taking your dog's food preferences into account when selecting treats, it is also important to keep in mind how easy the treats will be to (1) prepare, (2) carry around for training, (3) divide into appropriately-sized tiny training tidbits without leaving behind messy crumbs, and (4) give to your dog while training, as well as how many of the treats you can give during a training session without upsetting your dog's stomach or making him thirsty. Create a mix of several different treats your dog likes and you will have considerable flexibility when training. Because stress tends to reduce a dog's desire to eat, the ordinary dry treats that work well for training at home may not do the trick under the stress of training classes. Having some real meat or cheese options in your goodie bag will usually overcome the normal amounts of stress your dog may feel in class and allow you to use treats effectively there. For any type of dry treats you use, take a few moments before training to break them up into tiny pieces, toss them in a plastic baggie to keep your training bag or pocket clean, and you will be ready to train.

Less is more when using food as a training reward. A treat should simply be a *taste* of something special, not an entire meal in every bite! Similar to the human fast-food industry, the portion size of most pre-packaged dog treats is far larger than appropriate or necessary for use as training treats. Even for larger herding dogs, a treat reward should only be about the size of the tip of your little finger or a green pea. Your dog should be able to eat his treat in a second or two, with little, if any, chewing required. By keeping the treat size small, you will be able to train longer before your dog gets bored with the treat or actually gets physically full. You can also use richer, more calorie-dense treats without upsetting his stomach or causing him to gain weight. If you use raw foods as treats, be sure to handle them carefully to avoid spreading food-borne illnesses. To minimize potential spoilage problems, freeze tiny training-session portions so you can thaw and use up the entire portion in one session. If you are using cheese sticks, cut each stick into several sections and only take one section out of the refrigerator at a time. Regardless of the treats you are using, be sure to remove any leftovers from your pockets after training to protect your clothes from dog teeth and your washing machine from a gooey mess!

*This one pre-packaged treat can easily be broken into two dozen training-sized treats.*

## Toys and play

Toys and play are also potentially powerful rewards for herding dogs if they are used correctly, particularly for those dogs who aren't highly food-motivated. Think outside the traditional toy box when identifying potential training toys; they can be just about anything you and your dog can safely interact with together. Just because you wouldn't think of an item as a toy doesn't mean your dog won't see it as the greatest thing in the world to play with. Pay attention to the objects your dog chooses to play with on his own. Not all of them will be well suited to use for training, but you might find a few options. Your dog is in charge of toy selection—your job is to be sure the toy can be used safely and that the toy is only used under your supervision.

Most herding dogs are interested in toys that move. Balls, tug toys, and other toys that can be moved around in an erratic manner are all potentially good toy choices. Hard toys (Nylabones® and other hard plastic toys) are not appropriate for training rewards because you may toss the toy toward your dog to deliver it to him and if he catches a it, his teeth may be damaged. And if he doesn't catch it, he may be hit in the face and get hurt or scared. Give your dog hard toys to chew on between training sessions, and use soft plastic, fabric, fleece, or rubber toys for training.

When making your training toy selection, keep in mind how easy the toy will be to (1) carry and conceal from your dog during training, (2) hold on to while your dog plays with it, and (3) use once your dog covers it in drool. Expect that your dog will destroy a few toys over his lifetime. Toys are meant to be enjoyed, so buy some inexpensive ones with little or no stuffing and don't worry if they are worn out or destroyed during training.

When you play with toys as training rewards, you must be able to control the play so your dog doesn't grab his toy and run away from you, prematurely ending his training session. No matter how valuable the toy is for your dog and how hard he will work to get it, it is pointless to use it as a reward if your dog takes off the first time you give it to him and then plays keep away from you. That may be very fun for him, but it ruins your training session. If you are using a toy as a reward and your dog will try to take off with it, either the toy or your herding dog must be on a leash at all times so you can keep control of the situation. For example, if your dog absolutely loves tennis balls but doesn't have a reliable retrieve, either train him on a long line (twenty feet long or more) so you can let him chase his ball and then use the long line to guide him back to you if he tries to run away, or poke a hole through a tennis ball and thread a long piece of rope through it so you can get your dog to return it by reeling in the ball with the rope. Either way, you will be able to use the ball as a reward and, with minimal disruption, do several training repetitions without having your dog run away with it.

Allowing herding dogs to tug on their toys sometimes receives a bad rap because owners worry their dogs will become aggressive or try to "take charge" if they manage to get possession of the toy. Tugging itself is not the problem; how the game is played determines whether the game is appropriate for your dog. As long as you can start and end the game safely and on your terms, it is an acceptable game and potential reward for your dog if he enjoys tugging. Just keep in mind that you do not want your dog to become so excited he can no longer think or listen to you when playing tug. Control the tempo of the play through your own body language—if you want to slow things down, quit moving around with the toy. Stand still and talk to your dog in a very calm voice. If you want to rev your dog up a little more, become more animated yourself and talk in a more excited voice. Keep the tugging low and slow. Your dog's feet should stay on the ground and you should move the toy around gradually, side to side, when your dog is tugging on it. You risk seriously injuring your dog's neck and spine if you pick him up off his feet while he is hanging on to the toy or if you snap his head around quickly. Be sure you actually let your dog tug for a few moments while you play. If you shove the toy in your dog's face, then yank it away as soon as your dog grabs at it, he will soon lose interest in the game because he isn't ever getting the chance to play with the toy.

*It is important to keep tug games low and slow to avoid causing your dog injury. Here Gabriel has all four feet on the ground, his topline is fairly level, and the tugging is slow and controlled.*

No dog enjoys having a toy shoved in his face repeatedly, particularly if it's not even a toy he likes. That's not playing with your dog—that's assaulting him! An easy way to invite your herding dog to play with any toy is to ask yourself "What would a sheep or cow do?" and then move his toy around accordingly. Mimic the motion of livestock slowly moving away from your dog in a controlled manner, standing ground and not moving at all as your dog approaches, and erratically bolting away when chased too quickly. Your dog is hardwired to be aroused by these types of movements, so the more you can make a toy act like a herd animal, the more likely your herding dog will be interested in it. This type of play requires you to be actively involved in the game, too. Playing with your dog will help your relationship tremendously. You will have the opportunity to work on any bite-inhibition issues that may exist, teach your dog self-control, and reinforce the idea that you will provide all the fantastic stuff in your dog's life, including his toys. Besides that, it's just plain fun to play with your dog!

## Verbal and physical interaction

Most of the rewards your herding dog receives for performing the behaviors y him can originate from you. Because you will always have your hands and y available when you are interacting with your dog, it is definitely worth the time and effort it takes to identify ways to talk to and touch your dog to motivate and reward him for correct behavior.

Verbal interaction with your dog can be a powerful reward, if you take the time to build value into your voice. Humans are verbal creatures and talk to their dogs as if they are also human. Because he hears you all the time, your everyday voice is not very special to your dog. Verbal rewards are only effective if you change the pitch, tone, or presentation of your voice so it stands out against the daily verbal barrage your dog experiences. Higher-pitched sounds delivered in a quiet manner often catch a herding dog's ear, presumably because these sounds are similar to prey sounds. Verbally praising your dog in a different pitch than normal will help your praise stand out against the background noise. This does not mean you have to "baby talk" or be dramatic, just change the pitch a little to make it different from your everyday voice when you praise. Pair other types of rewards with praise to build even more value into the sound of your voice as a training reward.

You can also influence your dog's emotional state by the way you talk to him. For example, if you say "Good dog!!" in a high-pitched, upbeat manner, your dog will probably act excited by the praise. But if you say "G-o-o-o-d d-o-o-o-g" in a low-pitched, slow, drawn-out manner, your dog may very well start to relax. The speed and pitch of your praise needs to reflect the desired emotional response you want from your dog. Creating emotional associations with particular phrases and styles of praise can be very useful when you are training. Happy and excited praise can be used for active behaviors, such as coming when called, and soothing praise can be used for static behaviors, such as staying in one spot. The old adage "It's not *what* you say but *how* you say it" is very true in dog training, so experiment with your voice to find the styles that work best for various types of behaviors you want from your dog. Just remember not to be overly emotional or crazy with your cues; you don't want to have to resort to begging and carrying on to get your dog to respond to your cues when he is under stress.

Developing truly pleasurable forms of physical contact and play with herding dogs can be a little trickier than developing rewarding verbal skills. Although there are always individual exceptions, many herding dogs don't really seem to enjoy prolonged, stroking-type physical contact. However, there are many different ways to pet your dog. Watch him while you pet him. Does he really seem to enjoy the contact, or is he merely tolerating being petted? Lip licking, pinning his ears back, ducking slightly to avoid contact, and vigorous shaking after you get done petting him are all subtle signs of stress that suggest your dog may not really be enjoying the type of physical contact you are giving him. Experiment with various ways to pet your herding dog and watch his behavior closely to find out exactly how *he* enjoys being touched. You may find he enjoys being scratched at the base of the tail or behind the ears, but doesn't really enjoy being patted on the head or stroked down his back. You may also find that certain types of physical contact get him too excited to maintain self-control. Physical contact with your dog is a useful reward because as long as you have a hand free, you have a way to reward your dog.

## Environmental rewards

Treats, toys, praise, and pats are familiar rewards, but when you expand the definition of a reward to include *anything* in the environment your dog is willing to work for, your reward list becomes nearly limitless! The easiest way to develop a list of possible environmental rewards to use when training is simply to pay attention to what your dog likes to do when he's just hanging out, "being a dog." Going outside, sniffing pee-mail at the corner fire hydrant, digging a hole at the beach, sleeping on the sofa, and a myriad of other interactions with the environment can all potentially be used as rewards when you are training your herding dog. For example, if you cue your dog to give you eye contact when you are out for a walk and he looks at you, you can immediately release him and give him your cue to go read his pee-mail as his reward. Allowing your dog time to simply be a dog and do what he chooses to do (as long as you make sure it is safe) is very motivating and can be a powerful reward. It also provides a mental health boost for your dog. No matter how well trained he is, your dog is still a dog and needs a chance to just be a dog sometimes. As long as you can control your dog's access to what he wants so he only gets it *after* he performs a correct behavior, and the item is safe for both you and your dog to interact with, you can theoretically use it as a reward.

You can use other trained behaviors as rewards, too. If your dog loves to retrieve tennis balls, you can cue him to sit and, as soon as he does, release him to retrieve a ball. Soon he will be as excited to sit as he is to retrieve, because he will associate the sit with the reward of being allowed to retrieve. This type of reward is particularly useful if you are training your herding dog for a competitive dog sport; you can string multiple sports-related behaviors together, using ones your herding dog really enjoys as rewards for ones he doesn't enjoy as much.

To help you communicate clearly and consistently to your dog exactly when he is allowed to have a particular environmental reward, come up with a cue for interacting with each one. For example, suppose your herding dog loves to "read pee-mail" left by other dogs at the corner fire hydrant. You have identified sniffing the hydrant as a potential reward because you know he really likes to sniff it. You can use this as an environmental reward because you can control his access to it as you walk past it, it is safe for him to interact with, and you have a way to "give" the hydrant to him as a reward for correct behavior, simply by allowing him to go over to it. When you are walking past the hydrant and are not using it as a reward, simply keep walking and don't allow your dog to go over to it. Hold the leash short and, if necessary, move farther away from the hydrant as you pass it so your dog doesn't get to sniff it.

However, when you want to use the hydrant as a reward, cue your dog for a behavior, then immediately after he performs the correct behavior, tell him "Good dog! Now go read your pee-mail!" and release him to sniff the hydrant. He may be confused at first, especially if you haven't usually been allowing him to sniff the hydrant. Go over to the hydrant with him and encourage him to sniff it. If you are consistent in saying nothing about the hydrant when you don't want him to sniff it and telling him to read his pee-mail when you want him to check it out, he will eventually understand the hydrant is only available to him when you give him permission to interact with it. You will be able to use the hydrant as a reward, instead of worrying that your dog will pull your arm off trying to get to it every time you walk past it. As an added bonus, if you actually let him sniff the hydrant occasionally, it won't be quite so interesting to him anymore. Forbidden objects are always more intriguing than ones that are more readily accessible. By using distractions as rewards, you can actually decrease the power some distractions hold over your dog.

Whatever training rewards you decide to use with your dog, they should not be freely accessible to him when he isn't actually working with you to earn them. For example, many dogs have free access to toys at home. If your dog can play with his favorite toys anytime he chooses simply by going to the toy box and picking one out, the value of those toys as training rewards is diminished. Why should your dog work for you to earn a toy if he can go get it anytime he wants it, without doing anything at all for you? Any toy you have identified as a possible training reward should be put away so your dog no longer has free access to it. He can still play with it, but only after he has done something for you in order to earn that toy. If you are working on teaching your dog to give you eye contact on cue, cue your dog to watch; then, if he gives you eye contact, give him his favorite toy to play with as his reward. Since absence makes the heart grow fonder, your dog will be quite willing to work for his toy, because he still wants it but no longer has free access to it. You can give your dog free access to hard chew toys, like Kongs®, sterilized bones, etc. all the time, because these are not safe to use as training rewards. Likewise, if you give your herding dog a tasty treat "just because" every time you pass by the treat jar regardless of what he is doing at the time you give him the treat, his motivation to do something you want him to do to earn that type of treat will rapidly fade. However, if you only give him a treat *after* he has done something you cue him to do, he will be much more motivated to work for you to earn his treat. Things that your dog can't access when he is alone in your yard are the most useful environmental rewards to use for training. Keeping all types of rewards scarce preserves their value as training tools and will keep your dog motivated to work with you to earn them. He can still enjoy all his favorite toys, treats, and environmental rewards, but only after he has performed a desired behavior for you in order to earn access to them.

## When should the reward be given?

The time interval between a behavior and its consequence is critical to effective dog training. The closer in time the consequence follows the behavior, the quicker your dog will understand the connection between the two. You need to be on your toes when you work with your dog. One of the easiest ways to improve your timing is to take the time to get organized *before* you start your training session. Have your rewards readily accessible before you start asking for behaviors. If you are using treats as rewards and can't get your hand in your pocket easily, keep them in a treat bag or put them in a bowl on a nearby table so you can grab them quickly. Have them cut into small pieces and ready to go. If you are using a toy as a reward, have it in your pocket, your waistband, or your armpit, ready to be tossed to your dog. If you are going to let your dog outside as his reward, make sure you are training near the door so you can immediately let him out. If you can't get to the rewards quickly or the dog does something spontaneously that you want to reward, you can always immediately reward him with praise and physical interaction for a job well done. Ideally, the reward should be given the split second the correct behavior is performed, and withheld immediately if the correct behavior is not performed. Realistically, delivering or withholding the reward within a few seconds of the behavior is still more than quick enough for most dogs to associate the consequence with the behavior they just performed.

## Where should the reward be given?

Dogs associate rewards and corrections most strongly with what they are doing at the very moment they receive them. It is important to pay attention to where you deliver rewards so you don't introduce extra behaviors or confusion into your training session. For example, if you are working on teaching your herding dog to sit and are using a treat as the reward for a correct performance, you should deliver the treat in a way that allows him to get it without standing. If you hold the treat away from your dog and he has to get up and walk a few steps to get it, you are rewarding the walking behavior more strongly than the sitting behavior, because your dog is actively walking at the precise moment he gets his treat. If you put the treat right down in front of his mouth so he can eat it while he is still sitting, you are more strongly rewarding the sit position, because he is sitting at the moment he gets his treat. If your dog is working at a distance from you, toss a reward to him while he is still at a distance from you, instead of calling him back to you to get his reward. If you don't have a tossable reward to use, praise him while he is still at a distance, and then go to him if you want to deliver another type of reward. Pay attention to where your dog is and what he is doing when he gets his reward; his position should reinforce what you are actually trying to teach him.

*Where you reward your dog influences his learning. Rewarding Gabriel while he is still sitting will help him learn the sit behavior faster than if he stands up before getting his reward.*

Environmental rewards can be a little trickier to deliver immediately following a desired behavior. Try to train near the reward so you can quickly deliver it to your dog following a desired behavior. For example, if you are using the fire hydrant as an environmental reward for eye contact, ask your dog for eye contact near the hydrant so he can quickly be released to sniff it if he looks at you. Be sure your dog is still performing the correct behavior at the moment you release him to go to any environmental reward that you can't actually hand to him yourself (e.g., the fire hydrant). There may be a little more time between behavior and consequence with some environmental rewards, but if you keep the time lapse as short as possible, your dog will soon associate his behavior with the consequence.

## How should rewards be delivered?

How you deliver rewards is also important. If possible, praise and touch your dog before and during the delivery of other types of rewards. This contact helps build up the idea in his mind that you are quite literally connected with every reward in the universe, no matter what form that reward comes in. For example, give your dog a light pat or a quick scratch behind the ears and some calm praise while you feed him his treat if he is near enough for you to do so. If you release him to get an environmental reward, praise him as he goes to it.

Match the duration of the reward to the effort your dog puts forth to perform the behavior. The longer your dog has to concentrate to perform a behavior, or the more difficult the behavior is for him to perform, the longer the reward delivery should last. Combining different types of rewards is an easy way to increase the length of time your dog is rewarded for his behavior; combine a small treat with lots of verbal praise and physical contact to prolong the reward. Make a treat reward last longer by breaking it into even smaller pieces and feeding them to him one at a time. Aim to mark very special efforts with a full thirty seconds of continuous reward to maximize the impact of the reward on your dog's behavior. This type of special reward session is often called a **jackpot**; think of it as the canine equivalent of being given a bonus for working extra hard on a special project at work. Jackpots should be used sparingly, just for those special moments when your dog has had a training breakthrough or performed a behavior phenomenally well. Since most people aren't good at guessing how long thirty seconds really is, sing the Final Jeopardy song from the TV game show *Jeopardy!* to yourself while you reward your dog (or sing it aloud if that makes you and your dog happier!).

## Unpredictable rewards

The type of training reward your dog will earn from you should not be predictable. He should only be able to predict that he will get something he wants from you *after* he performs a correct behavior for you, but the reward itself should become variable over time. If you use treats to reward your dog after every correct behavior when he is in the first stage of learning, you should begin to introduce other types of rewards, including praise, as he starts to gain fluency with that particular behavior. If you continue to give him a treat every time he executes the behavior, his consistency may suffer if he does not see that treat in your hand or smell it in your pocket. Through excessive repetitions, he has associated the presence of a treat as part of the cue itself. If you cue him to perform the behavior without the treat and he doesn't perform it, it may be because you unintentionally changed your cue (from your dog's point of view) when you eliminated holding the treat in your hand, and now he is genuinely confused about what you expect him to do. It is not because he will only perform for treats, but rather he has strongly linked the presence of the treat with the cue itself and he doesn't know what you want him to do when you take the treat away. However, if you start to vary the types of rewards you give him for a correct performance as soon as he has learned the behavior, he won't consider treats to be part of the cue. This will keep him interested and working hard to obtain his rewards, since he never knows if he is going to earn a super-duper environmental reward, a tasty treat, a nice-feeling butt scratch, or simply sincere praise for his efforts. Only two things will be predictable for your dog: (1) you will always reward acceptable behavior, even if that reward is simply praise or the opportunity to continue to work; and (2) you will be unpredictable in the type of reward he receives for a job well done.

## Why go through all this work to identify rewards?

To consistently perform any learned behavior, your dog must be physically and mentally capable of executing the behavior, thoroughly understand what you expect him to do, and be motivated enough by his potential reward to put the effort into performing the behavior every time he is asked to do so. Take the time to figure out what *your* herding dog is motivated to work for so you can mix and match behaviors and rewards to keep his motivation to work with you at a high level. The harder the behavior is for your dog to perform, the more desirable the reward should be for a correct performance. Keep your dog guessing what he will earn for his effort by varying the rewards you use to keep his learned behaviors strong long after formal training classes end.

# Chapter 7

## Management and Training for No-Nonsense Attitude, The Urge to Take Control, and Low Frustration Threshold

---

*The shepherd is the brain behind the dog's brain,*
*But his control of dog, like dog's of sheep,*
*Is never absolute—that's the beauty of it.*

*Cecil Day Lewis*
*Irish poet*

Herding dogs tend to be type-AAA, card-carrying control nuts. Anything that moves should be chased down and controlled, and they appoint themselves to do the chasing and controlling. They also tend to be rather aloof toward dogs and people they don't know, sometimes to the point of being socially inappropriate, and can easily become frustrated around anything they can't get to that moves too much or makes too much noise. These traits can be exceptionally problematic if your herding dog decides he needs to control something that doesn't *want* to be controlled; biting people, chasing cars, or getting into dogfights can result when your dog doesn't have appropriate self-control. Exhibiting self-control is critical for your herding dog if he is to live a bite-free, fight-free life.

This chapter contains many management techniques and training exercises to help your dog resist the urge to take control. Remember, management techniques don't actually teach your dog *how* to behave. They simply prevent him from acting inappropriately in the first place. The training exercises will actually *teach* your dog to demonstrate more self-control, even in exciting situations, by giving him acceptable alternative behaviors to perform.

# Management techniques

## Respect the bubble

Preventing your dog from losing self-control can be easily accomplished by protecting your dog's personal space. Your dog's personal space is the amount of space he needs between him and something exciting or threatening, to remain calm and under your control. Dogs, people, bicycles, small animals, and cars are just a few things that might overly excite your dog if he gets too close to them. An easy way to visualize your dog's personal space is to imagine him moving through his environment encased in a bubble. If his bubble is intact, he can ignore distractions, listen to you, and respond to your cues. However, if his bubble is popped because the distraction gets too close, your dog will stop responding to your cues and start to lose self-control. His instincts will begin to take over and his learned behaviors will deteriorate. Respecting the bubble and giving your dog the space he needs is the simplest way to reduce and, in some cases, eliminate many problem behaviors your herding dog may display in public.

The size of your dog's bubble may vary, depending on the type of distraction involved, his experiences with it, and the amount of training he has already received to help him maintain self-control around that particular distraction. By teaching your dog to pay attention to you even when you are near distractions, you can eventually make all of his bubbles very small, meaning he will learn to exhibit self-control even when he is very close to distractions.

A simple way to identify the initial size of your dog's bubbles around different distractions is to take a few information-gathering walks with him. These walks are not training walks *per se;* these walks are to help you determine how much distance your dog needs in order to remain calm around things that arouse him. Watch for all the things that catch your dog's attention and note how close you are when he first starts focusing on them. Identify your dog's bubbles in training classes, at the vet's office, and anywhere else you go with him. If he gets excited and tunes you out at home, identify his home bubbles as well. Make a list of these bubbles to refer to in the future as a reminder. This list will also serve as a yardstick to measure the progress you make in shrinking the bubbles through training. Prioritize the bubbles, so you can start working on the ones that are most common or problematic for your dog first. Identifying and prioritizing your dog's bubbles around everyday distractions is the first step in helping him learn to exhibit self-control and behave in a more acceptable manner around them.

*Think of the amount of personal space your dog needs as a bubble that you must protect if you want your herding dog to remain calm and able to listen to you around distractions.*

## Defensively driving your driver

Once you have identified your dog's various bubbles, you need to start protecting them through defensive doggie driving. When you take your dog out for a walk, the largest bubble you have identified will determine how far ahead you need to proactively scan the environment for distractions. If your dog gets frustrated about approaching dogs when they are still two blocks away from you, and that is his largest bubble, you need to be scanning proactively at least *three* blocks ahead for other dogs moving toward you. This will give you time to see an approaching dog, decide what you need to do to protect your dog's bubble, and actually start doing it—all *before* your dog's two-block bubble is burst and he starts going bonkers, trying to get to the other dog. This is a habit that takes time to develop; most people don't look very far ahead when they walk. Think of proactive scanning as being similar to good defensive-driving techniques; you need to walk with your head up, looking forward and scanning the environment as you walk, just as you look ahead and scan the roads when you are driving your car. An added benefit of looking farther ahead when you walk is you will appear to walk with more confidence. Herding dogs are masters at reading body language and when you walk looking ahead of you, your herding dog will have more confidence in your guidance. If, instead, you look at your feet when you walk, you will appear to lack confidence. You will have no way to effectively protect your dog's bubble from dogs or anything else that gets him aroused because you won't see what's ahead of you in time to respond appropriately.

*Ami confidently walks her Australian Shepherd Tazer through the neighborhood, looking ahead to protect his distraction bubbles and prevent problems from occurring.*

Defensive doggie driving doesn't just apply when you are out for a walk. When you take your dog into a training class or the vet's office, keep your dog's leash short and your eyes looking ahead. Scan the room before entering and locate the best place to go with your dog. Walk with confidence into the room and go immediately to the spot you pick out. You may not be able to find all the space you need to protect your dog's bubble completely in every situation, but you will certainly help your dog's behavior by picking the best option available to you and confidently filling that space with you and your dog.

## Right-of-way rules

Sidewalks are the bane of many people's evening strolls through the neighborhood with their dogs. Those straight, smooth concrete lines seem to suck all the common sense out of dog walkers when it comes to preventing unpleasant or uncontrolled encounters between leashed dogs. Canine social rules decree that strange dogs approach one another in an arcing manner, slowly and calmly, bodies soft, eyes usually averted, checking one another out by sniffing rear ends before assessing each other head-on. However, sidewalks, leashes, and owners usually prevent this greeting ritual from happening. Dog owners sometimes stick to that straight sliver of concrete as if physically attached to it, forcing dogs to approach each other head-on, allowing them to strain against their leashes to get to each other, preventing the dogs from doing anything remotely resembling a proper canine greeting. Dogs may get excited or become scared in these situations, leading to confrontations that could be completely avoided if one dog owner would simply give the right-of-way to the other by taking his dog off the sidewalk and moving as far away as necessary to proactively protect his own dog's bubble. This may seem like an obvious thing to do, but few people take this simple step to prevent outbursts from happening.

Although it may be difficult at first to remember to yield the right-of-way to distractions, once you see how many embarrassing meetings you prevent with this simple technique, you will become motivated to make adjustments to your walking routine. If there is a dog in the neighborhood who gets your dog excited by running along the fence as you walk, walk on the other side of the street when you pass that house, or take a different route altogether until you have taught your herding dog to ignore the dog behind the fence. If your dog struggles to remain calm while passing other dogs, cross the street, make an about-turn and go back in the direction you came from, or step off the curb and have your dog remain stationary near you while another dog passes. Never force a head-on confrontation.

When you alter your path to avoid distractions, turn with confidence and authority, then step out at a brisk pace in your new direction. Ideally, if your timing is good and you scan far enough ahead on your walk, your dog should not be distressed by the sudden change in your route. The key with this technique is to be confident in your body language and voice as you change direction. Your dog may associate the oncoming distraction with any tenseness in your body or voice and get even more excited or worried about the oncoming distraction, unless you act unconcerned and nonchalant about it as you change direction. Talk to your dog in a calm, conversational tone as you walk away. If your dog likes treats, offer him a few as you move away, but only if he is walking with you and not straining to turn back to the distraction. You want to reward walking away with you, not looking back at the distraction. Don't nag your dog or yell at him if he keeps turning around. If he reacts to the distraction at all, it is a sign that *you* waited too long to try to avoid the situation and his bubble for that distraction was popped. Just continue to walk away with confidence. Eventually there will be enough distance between your herding dog and the distraction to allow him to regain his composure. Distance is always your friend. You will never go wrong if you calmly and promptly increase the distance between your dog and anything that arouses him.

As your herding dog learns how to remain calm around distractions and his bubbles start to shrink through training, you won't need to make as many detours in your walking path. But until your dog learns new coping skills, walk the few extra steps it takes to yield the right-of-way and keep your dog out of the path of oncoming trouble, then pat yourself on the back for being a responsible, proactive dog owner, and remind yourself you've also just added a few extra steps to your dog's daily exercise quota as a bonus!

## Keep calm and move on

At the outbreak of World War II, the British Ministry of Information created a series of motivational posters to bolster British morale if the Germans ever invaded the island. One poster displayed the simple statement "Keep calm and carry on." This notion can certainly apply to many dog training situations, too! Sometimes you have no choice but to walk close to something that will get your herding dog overly excited. Sometimes your dog will see a bicycle before you do. Sometimes you will encounter something new with your dog and he will have an unexpected initial reaction to it. Sometimes life happens in spite of your best intentions and your dog's bubble is burst. When this happens and your dog gets aroused or starts acting out, it is very important that you just keep calm and move on. It is not always easy to do, but this will minimize the trauma and drama of the situation for both you and your dog.

*When something unexpected happens, keep as calm as possible, keep your feet moving, and get your dog out of the situation as quickly as you can.*

When a person gets excited or nervous, many physical and physiological changes occur; body posture, breathing patterns, voice tone and inflection, and hormone levels can all change without a person even really being aware of the changes. Herding dogs can easily sense these subtle changes that occur when your adrenaline starts flowing. If you are upset, it is likely your dog will get upset as well. Although it is impossible to fool your dog completely, you can certainly minimize the impact your emotions have on your dog's behavior by making a conscious effort to keep calm. If your dog's bubble is burst or something unexpected happens and your dog loses control, take a deep breath, straighten your shoulders, stand tall, and then calmly and quickly get your dog out of the situation. Don't yell at your dog or try to reason with him about his behavior (do you really think he understands you when you tell him the other dog does not want to be bossed around?). Keep your voice calm and quiet and keep your feet moving. A quiet voice is often more confident sounding than a loud one. If you maintain a façade of calm authority, it will help you get out of a difficult situation with a minimum of difficulty. And if you keep moving, you will also reduce the length of time the situation lasts.

## Be your dog's advocate

Taking responsibility for your herding dog's safety and well-being is an important part of being a loving dog owner. Sometimes that responsibility requires you to tell other people that their dogs can't interact with your dog. When herding dogs are puppies, they need as much safe exposure as possible to people and socially appropriate dogs of all ages, shapes, sizes, colors, and both sexes. They need to meet dogs who will play with them and dogs who will tell them (appropriately) to go away. However, not every dog you meet in the neighborhood has the proper social skills to teach your puppy these important lessons. As adults, herding dogs usually prefer their personal space not be invaded, particularly by overly friendly, socially inept, quick-moving dogs, as well as by people they don't know. You need to accept responsibility for protecting your herding dog, whatever his age, from potentially unsafe situations.

Never assume a person knows how to approach your dog safely, will keep his dog under control, or see anything wrong with how his dog is acting. If your dog is approached by a person who is moving too fast or trying to get down in your dog's face, don't allow that person access to your dog. Remember, no one has the right to touch your dog without your permission. If need be, step between the person and your dog to prevent contact. Children can be particularly troublesome for herding dogs because of their fast motions, high-pitched voices, and shorter height that often places the child's face even with the dog's face. If someone asks if his dog can say "hi" to your dog, politely decline if you suspect the greeting will cause problems for your dog. Explain that your dog is learning good greeting manners, so you need to pass on the meeting; that should deter the other owner from approaching. Unfortunately, some dog owners can't talk and keep their dogs close to them at the same time! Be sure to watch the other dog while this conversation is going on, to make sure the dog doesn't pull too close to yours. Never be afraid to ask another dog owner to call his dog away, either. Even if the owner says "It's okay—my dog is friendly!" that doesn't give his dog the right to assault your dog (nor should *you* say that to someone else and then allow *your* dog to pull over to another dog without permission). The other owner has already failed to realize that this situation isn't just about his dog; there are, in fact, *two* dogs involved in the situation and *both* dogs have a say in how safe the encounter will be. Don't allow another owner to put your dog in a potentially dangerous situation. You will be doing your dog a huge favor if you prevent close encounters with unknown dogs from happening.

Being your herding dog's advocate also applies to choosing places to take your dog. Do not take your dog into a situation you know he isn't ready to handle yet or one you can't manage well enough to prevent him from behaving inappropriately. For example, many pet stores allow you to take leashed pets in with you to shop. Such stores are full of narrow aisles, with limited visibility, and lots of exciting sights and smells. The floors are usually slick and difficult to walk on without slipping. Some shoppers are pushing carts, while others are walking their own dogs with varying degrees of success. Most shoppers and store employees assume that if a dog is brought into the store, he is friendly with all people and all dogs and will try to interact with him. This can be a very stressful situation for your herding dog. Bringing him into this type of situation without first teaching him how to cope successfully with that level of stress is asking for trouble. It would be far more prudent to leave your dog at home when you go out to buy dog food until you have taught him how to maintain self-control and behave appropriately in highly distracting environments. If you repeatedly overwhelm your dog by putting him in situations he isn't able to handle, you will give him more practice with the unacceptable behaviors you want to change and make the task of changing those behaviors more difficult. You will also teach him that he can't really trust you to keep him safe, so he has no other choice than to follow his instincts and try to control the situation himself. If you are selective about the situations you place your dog in and gradually increase the distractions your dog must deal with as he learns how you expect him to behave, before long you will end up with a dog that you can take just about anywhere and one that other people would like to have!

## Keep 'em busy

Sometimes you have no choice but to keep your dog in a stressful environment, such as the vet's office or a training class, in close proximity to distractions. When this happens, keep your dog busy interacting with you to help him remain as calm as possible. If you don't keep your dog's attention on you, he will find something to pay attention to on his own, and it probably won't be you. You need to actively engage your dog to keep him from fixating on distractions in his environment. If you attend training classes, you must focus on your dog from the moment you pull into the parking lot until the moment you leave. Walking at the end of a six-foot leash is always a privilege, *never* a right for your dog. Keep your dog on a very short leash (but keep it loose enough that you aren't strangling him!) as you enter and leave the training building, to keep him as close as possible to you and help him keep his focus on you while you are moving. Once you take your seat, continue engaging him so he will pay more attention to you than to other dogs in class. A sterilized hollow bone filled with peanut butter, wet dog food, or squeeze cheese and then frozen may be a great distractor for your dog, as long as he is calm enough to eat. Tricks or basic obedience commands will also keep your herding dog focused more on you than on the other dogs in the class; just be sure your dog's activities aren't too distracting for his classmates. It takes considerable effort to keep your dog focused on you for an entire training class. However, if you prevent him from getting overly excited or frustrated, you will both be able to listen and learn more in class.

*Because Melissa taught her Miniature American Shepherd Treo how to touch a target with her nose, she always has a handy behavior to use in distracting situations to keep Treo's focus on working with her.*

## Training exercises

Now that you have a selection of management techniques to make some quick behavioral fixes, you are ready to teach your dog how you actually expect him to behave in frustrating, distracting situations. Remember that thoroughly training any behavior takes time and you will need to increase the intensity of the distractions you train your dog around gradually, as he develops behavioral fluency. To deal with the no-nonsense, take-control attitude and low frustration threshold your herding dog may have, you need to teach him to exhibit a higher degree of self-control than he normally would if left to act on his own instincts.

## That'll do

**Exercise Goal:** Your herding dog will stop his current behavior when he is given a release cue.

One approach to teaching self-control is to teach your dog a release cue. A release cue is used to tell your dog to stop doing whatever he is doing at the moment. He must display a high level of self-control to quit performing a behavior he wants to continue performing when you give him your cue to stop. The herding cue "That'll do" historically meant a dog should stop whatever work he was doing, leave the livestock, and come back to the shepherd. If you choose to use this phrase as your release cue, it will simply mean your dog should stop performing whatever behavior he is doing at the moment. This cue is taught in conjunction with other cues, so there are not steps, *per se,* for teaching the release cue. Just apply your release cue to every behavior you teach your dog and he will soon learn when he is supposed to stop working.

1. Pick a unique word or short phrase that will indicate to your dog that he should stop performing whatever behavior he is doing when he hears it. "Free," "Break," "All done," and "That'll do" are all examples of a release cue. Have several really valuable rewards ready to use. These might be super tasty treats, a favorite toy, or the chance to do some other behavior right away that your dog enjoys.

2. Cue your dog to perform a basic behavior, such as sit. When he sits, praise him calmly for sitting. If he gets up while you are praising him, quickly and quietly help him back into the sit position. Pause for a second or two while your dog continues to sit, then give him the release cue "That'll do" in an enthusiastic, upbeat manner, and quickly step away from your dog. Move away, clap your hands, smile, and act as if you truly do want your dog to get up. He may be hesitant to get up at first, so be sure to be inviting with your body as well as your voice. If he absolutely refuses to budge, you may need to lure him a few times by tossing a treat or toy in front of him as you give him his release cue, to convince him it really is okay to move out of position. Repeat five times per training session and be sure your dog gets completely up out of his sit when you give him his release cue.

3. Use your release cue to end every behavior you cue your dog to perform. This gives him a definite ending for his behavior. If your dog anticipates being released and ends his behavior early, quickly and quietly help him do the behavior again, wait a few seconds, and then release him with your release cue. For example, if he gets up from a sit before you release him, put him back into a sit where he was originally sitting, wait a few seconds, and then, if he is still sitting, give his release cue. If he was walking at your side and pulled in front of you before you released him, get him back next to you, walk a few steps with him beside you, and then

release him. Resist the urge to blurt out your release cue if you see your dog starting to break position. That isn't teaching your dog to wait for his release cue; that is your dog training you to say your release cue whenever he decides he wants to quit performing for you! Teaching your dog to have self-control requires you to have self-control, too.

4. If, instead of stopping a behavior before you release him, your dog starts fixating on performing the behavior and won't stop when you give your release cue, you may need to physically interrupt the behavior to help him stop. This sometimes happens with moving behaviors that resemble instinctual herding behaviors; your dog wants to keep working at all costs. Remember, responding to your cues needs to be more valuable to your dog than continuing the behavior he is performing, or he won't be motivated to stop when you tell him to stop. Sometimes the most effective reward to give your dog for listening to you and stopping a behavior on a release cue is to immediately cue him to go back to the behavior he did not want to stop performing in the first place. Over time, your dog will learn that listening to you doesn't automatically mean his opportunity to work will end, and it will gradually become easier for him to listen to you and disengage from any behavior on cue.

Teaching your dog when to stop performing a behavior is just as important as teaching him how to perform the behavior in the first place. Herding dogs sometimes take their work a little too seriously; anticipate this possible problem by using a release cue with every other cue you use to teach your dog how to turn on and off to working with you!

## Stop and drop

**Exercise Goal:** Your herding dog will immediately lie down on a verbal cue regardless of his location relative to you.

All dogs have the predatory instinct to chase things that move, but careful breeding has greatly enhanced that instinct in herding dogs. Unfortunately, this instinct doesn't naturally discriminate between livestock and other moving objects. Herding dogs may try to chase or herd inappropriate, and sometimes dangerous, moving things, like cars, bicycles, and running children. Teaching your dog to drop into a down immediately might save his life someday by preventing him from running headlong into a dangerous situation.

1. For this exercise, your dog needs to understand how to lie down from a stand without sitting first; this is the quickest way for him to drop. Most dogs are taught to sit and then lie down. If your dog already knows how to lie down from a stand without sitting first, you can skip ahead to Step 2. If not, the first thing to teach your dog is the sphinx-like down or splat-like down. Be sure to put your dog on leash and have some exceptionally tasty treats handy before starting this exercise. Stand your

dog beside you, facing the same direction you are facing. If your dog is standing on your left side, hold a treat in your right hand. If your dog is standing on your right side, hold a treat in your left hand. Kneel down beside your dog so you can help him lie down without towering over him and possibly intimidating him; the two of you should still be facing the same direction, parallel to each other. Show your dog the treat and encourage him to nibble on it as you move your hand very slowly down, at an angle, to a spot between your dog's front feet, slightly underneath him. At the same time, put your free hand on your dog's shoulders and, while your treat hand moves slowly to the floor, gently slide your hand along his back at the same angle. Don't press straight down on your dog's back or physically try to force him into a down; that will cause him to brace against the push and stand firm. The pressure you are putting on his back is simply to help him ease down into the correct position and not leave his rump sticking up in the air as he would in a play bow. The pressure needs to be at a slight downward angle toward his rump so he "folds" into the sphinx position. If he sits instead of lying down, get him back up into a stand and start over. Once both ends of your dog are completely on the floor, reward your dog with the remainder of the treat, some calm praise, and slow, soothing strokes along his back. Delay giving him his release cue for a few seconds so he learns right from the start to hold this position until he is released. As he begins to understand how to lie down in this manner, vary how long you delay before you give him his release cue. Keep him guessing or he may try to anticipate his release. Do five repetitions per training session.

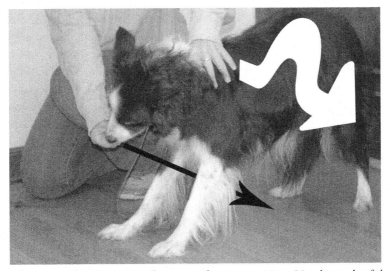

*Don't use your hands to try to force your dog into position. Use the angle of the treat lure to get your dog to start shifting his weight back and dropping his head down, and your hand on his back to remind him to drop the other end, too.*

2.  Once your dog lies down as soon as you start moving your hand toward the floor, eliminate the treat in your hand as a lure to get your dog to lie down. If you stick with the treat lure too long, it may be difficult to get the behavior later without a treat in your hand. Begin to fade the treat by doing a few repetitions of the down using the treat as a lure and then immediately cueing a repetition without a treat in your hand. If you hold your hand in the same position and move your hand in the same way you did when you were holding a treat, your dog should complete the drop even though you do not actually have a treat. Praise, then get a treat out of your pocket or treat bag, give it to your dog while he is still lying down, and release him. Once he will drop without the lure, resist the urge to go back to it if your dog doesn't drop; instead, quietly help him lie down with your hand cue and gentle strokes along his back. If you haven't rushed your training, he should start to fold down as soon as you start to pet him along his back. Continue to move your hand at the same speed and in the same manner toward the floor as you did when you first started teaching this behavior.

3.  As soon as your dog will lie down without any physical assistance from you at least 80% of the time, you are ready to start standing up while cueing him to lie down. Until now, you have been kneeling beside him when you cued him to lie down, so he needs to learn that you may give him the cue when you are standing up, too. Stand beside him and bend over at the waist as you cue him to lie down; be sure to point all the way to the floor, as you did in the previous step. Eventually, your dog will start to lie down without your reaching so far toward the floor. Use the 80% rule from Chapter 5 to help you determine when your dog is ready for you to change positions again and stand more upright as you are giving him your cue. Before you try to stand completely upright, you should be able to cue your dog to lie down without needing to touch the floor. Only reward quick drops with a treat. If you reward slow drops, you are teaching your dog that it is acceptable for him to be slow. If your dog slowly lowers himself to the floor, release him without giving him a treat and immediately cue him to lie down again. Reward him if this drop is quicker. If it isn't, you may need to go back to kneeling beside him for a few more sessions before trying to start standing up again. And don't forget to have him hold his position until you give him your release cue. If he gets up before you release him, quietly put him back in a down exactly where he was supposed to be staying, wait a few seconds, and then give him the release cue before he gets up on his own again. When you can stand upright and your dog will drop quickly and completely at your side, you can add a verbal cue, such as "Splat," while you give your hand cue toward the floor.

4.  Now you can begin to teach your dog to lie down no matter where he is relative to you. Dogs are awesome discriminators. Just because your dog will reliably drop at your side does not mean he will drop if he is facing you; the view he has of you when he is at your side is very different from the view he has of you when he is facing you. You need to help him generalize the drop behavior to other positions relative to you because when you really need him to lie down immediately, he probably isn't going to be at your side.

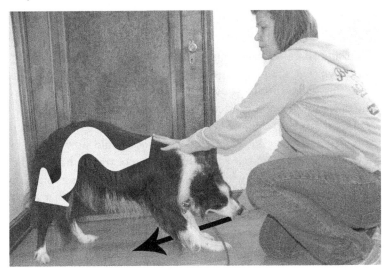

*Use a barrier behind your dog to keep him from moving away from you while you teach him to lie down in front of you.*

Start this step with your dog standing in front of you, facing you. Use a wall or other physical barrier behind him to keep him from backing away from you; you should be just far enough away from the barrier to allow your dog to lie down without touching it. Kneel down in front of him so you don't have to loom over him if he needs help lying down. It will be a little more awkward for you to help him lie down when the two of you are set up like this, so be sure he really does understand how to lie down beside you before you start this step to minimize the number of times you need to physically help him lie down when he is in front of you. Cue him to "Splat" while moving your hands as you did in Step 1 to help him lie down. You will have to bend over him when you do this, so be gentle and quiet while you help him. If he has thoroughly learned "Splat" at your side, you shouldn't have to help him too many times before he starts lying down on his own in front of you. As soon as he is at least 80% reliable performing on cue while you are kneeling, start cueing the behavior while you are standing upright. Remember to always pair this cue with his release cue, and vary how long you wait before releasing him to keep him guessing how long he will have to hold his position. If he gets up before you've released him, immediately put him back into the down in the exact spot he chose to leave and start again. Start out asking him to hold his down for just a few seconds before giving your release cue, and gradually build up to longer periods of time as his understanding of the behavior improves.

5.  When your dog is reliably lying down when he is facing you, the last basic position to teach him is to "Splat" when he is facing away from you. This can be difficult for two reasons. First, your dog isn't looking directly at you, so he can't see all the little body cues you have probably been subconsciously giving him to help him perform the behavior up to this point. Even though dogs have better peripheral vision than humans, your dog will still miss some of your body language when he is facing directly away from you. Second, your dog is now facing the rest of the world and there is a lot to be distracted by out there, so be sure to start this step in a quiet environment. Your dog should now be reliably performing "Splat" beside you as well as in front of you, so he should quickly learn to lie down even when he is facing away from you. Start this step with your dog in front of you, facing the same direction that you are facing (i.e., he is seeing the same view you are seeing). Cue him to "Splat," then quietly and gently help him into position by stroking him along his back with gentle, downward pressure. He should drop straight down into position rather than turning toward you. Even though turning around to face you before dropping may seem desirable, it will slow down his drop. The goal here is an almost immediate drop to the ground when your dog hears your drop cue. He can turn his head back to look at you, but his body should remain facing away. Don't forget to give him your release cue before he decides to get up. If he anticipates your release, quietly put him back down in the spot he left and have him hold the down position briefly before giving him his release cue. You can also teach him to drop behind you and at various angles facing toward you and away from you to further develop his understanding of the drop cue. Be ready to help him complete the behavior by gently and quietly guiding him into a down if he does not respond promptly on his own. To keep your drop cue strong, don't give him the cue if you can't help him complete the behavior.

*Gabriel has learned to listen for a verbal cue to lie down, and to lie down without turning his body around, for a very quick drop.*

6.   The last component to add to the "Splat" is distractions. Gradually ask your dog to lie down while increasing the level of distractions. Always train with a leash or long line on your dog so you can prevent him from breaking his position and running after the distraction you are working around, or simply walking away if he isn't motivated enough to continue working with you. You should also start giving him rewards other than treats for dropping on cue. Praise, allowing him to check out his environment, or the opportunity to do some other behavior he enjoys can all be very motivating rewards for quick drops. When he is 80% reliable dropping from different stationary positions relative to you with distractions around, he is ready to begin the Moving Stop and Drop exercise.

## Moving stop and drop

**Exercise Goal:** Your herding dog will immediately stop and lie down on cue when in motion.

Herding dogs are quick, athletic dogs. Before you even realize what is going on, your dog can be running full out in an attempt to overtake and herd a child, a car, or another animal. Teaching a running dog to stop and lie down can literally be a lifesaver. Before you start this exercise, be sure your dog understands how to lie down from a stand in any position relative to you with distractions around, as outlined in the Stop and Drop exercise.

1. Start with your dog on a six-foot leash, facing you. Practice a few stationary downs to get him thinking about the drop behavior before asking him to drop while moving. During this stationary warm-up, give him your verbal cue as well as pointing toward the ground with your hand, using a motion similar to the one you first used to lure him into the down. Have him hold his position a few seconds, then give him his release cue. Be sure he gets up on his release cue; if he doesn't, help him up out of the down as you did when you first taught him his release cue, by tossing a treat or toy in front of him when you release him.

2. After this stationary warm-up, face your dog and quickly take a few steps backward to get him moving toward you, as if you are calling him to you. Shorten his leash as he approaches; if he catches up with you quickly, don't worry. The closer he is to you the first few times you work on this step, the easier it will be to help him be successful. Stop abruptly in front of him, stand up straight, and give him the cue to "Splat." If he thoroughly understands the cue from the previous exercise, he should quickly begin to drop. Your body will be blocking his forward motion as he begins to drop. You want him to drop promptly, with little extra forward motion. Once he is lying down, facing you, reach down and reward him, then give him his release cue and let him get up. If your dog doesn't lie down completely, slowly and calmly reach over his back and gently stroke down it to get him to drop his entire body down. This will help him remember there is more to his body than just his front end. Complete five repetitions per training session.

3. When your dog is 80% reliable (accurate four out of five times) on a single cue right at your feet, you can start teaching him to lie down farther away on his path toward you. Start by cueing him to lie down when he is about twelve inches from you. If he tries to come closer before dropping, lean in to block him from walking forward before dropping. Using the 80% rule, gradually increase the distance between you and your dog when you give him his "Splat" cue. When he is able to lie immediately

down at the end of his six-foot leash, you can switch to using a long line so you can continue to increase the distance between the two of you. You may have to let your dog get interested in something else in the environment in order to move very far away from him; herding dogs have a pretty good sense of where their flock is at all times, even if they aren't looking directly at it. If your dog is not interested in anything but working with you, you can ask a helper to hold him while you move away, or put a tasty treat out for your dog to eat, so you can get a head start on backing away from him in order to get more distance between the two of you. Just remember that if you cue your dog to lie down, you need to be willing and able to help him successfully complete the behavior. If he fails to respond to your drop cue, it may be that you increased the distance too quickly. To minimize the chances he won't respond to your drop cue, increase the distance twelve inches at a time and be sure your dog honestly can pass the 80% test before adding more distance. Your dog's forward motion should stop as soon as you cue him to lie down.

4. You can also start cueing your dog to lie down while moving away from you. This is particularly useful if you need to stop your dog as he is running out the door or down the street chasing something. For this variation, start with your dog on leash out in front of you in a quiet environment. Allow him to become distracted by something in front of him (you may need to toss a toy or treat in front of him to get him to move in that direction). Walk close behind him and cue him to "Splat," without backing away from him. You want him to stay facing away from you in this step. If he does not immediately start to drop, gently help him into the position as you did with the stationary Stop and Drop exercise. Don't let him turn around or walk toward you. He should simply drop where he is. He can look over his shoulder at you, but his body shouldn't change directions. Reach in to reward him and then give him his release cue. Gradually let him get farther in front of you before you cue him to lie down.

5. As your dog gains fluency with the moving down behavior, be sure you aren't too predictable with the distance between the two of you when you give the "Splat" cue. Sometimes drop your dog very close to you; other times, drop him much farther away. Call him to you sometimes without dropping him at all. The less predictable you are, the more attention your herding dog is apt to give you. If you follow a set pattern, your dog will start to operate on autopilot every time you cue him and may start to drop at the distance you've been practicing, even if you didn't actually cue him to lie down.

6. Once your dog is 80% reliable dropping when he is twenty feet or more away from you, start adding in a few distractions. Balls being tossed or rolled, moving cars, running children, and anything else your dog is likely to try to herd are all distractions to train around after your dog understands the basic behavior. Always have him on a long line for this training and never encourage him to fixate on or chase after anything, or let him get close to any dangerous object. Your goal is to help your dog learn to listen to you and respond appropriately in real-life situations, even when his instincts are telling him to chase and herd something in his environment. Safety and common sense should guide the challenges you provide with this training. Protect your dog's bubbles for the things he is likely to chase so he remains calm enough to listen to you and respond appropriately.

## Walking in a straight line

**Exercise Goal:** To prevent your herding dog from trying to control your movement while you walk him on leash.

Whether your dog was bred to head or heel livestock, there is a certain circular aspect to how he naturally tends to move when he is in close proximity to anything he instinctively thinks should be herded (which may include you). When you are walking your dog, this herding behavior can be quite obvious (your dog literally runs circles around you as you walk) or extremely subtle (slowly arcing in behind or beside you to subtly guide you to move in a particular direction). Although there is no such thing as a completely straight line in nature, there are plenty of straight lines in urban environs that you and your dog must deal with every day. Teaching your dog to walk a reasonably straight line beside you when you have him on leash is a good way to make strolls down the sidewalk more pleasant for you and is also an important skill to teach your dog if you want to compete with him in competitive dog sports. This exercise also teaches your dog to walk on a loose leash, so it is well worth your time to work on this with him!

When you ask someone to name a dog-training tool, often the first one that comes to mind is a leash. Far too many dog owners use leashes to physically force their dogs to stay close while walking, instead of actually teaching the dogs where they are expected to walk, with or without a leash on. Using a leash as a physical restraint teaches your dog he doesn't need to pay attention to you when you go for a walk together; he is free to move around as he pleases until the leash stops him. A better way to use your dog's leash is as a canine fashion accessory and a leash law requirement. Teach your dog to walk beside you without using his leash to control him, so he will learn that it is his responsibility to pay attention to you and adjust his position based on your location, rather than a tight leash (but only if it is physically safe for you to work with him in this manner). The leash you use for this exercise should be long enough to loop around your waist or over your shoulder, or pass through a belt loop before attaching it to your dog's collar. Your dog needs to be safely attached to you in some way so you don't need to use your hands, but the leash should not put any tension on your dog's neck when he is walking politely beside you. A service dog leash is particularly useful for this exercise, but isn't necessary. If you need a longer leash, you can make a custom-length rope leash using supplies readily available from your local hardware store. Use common sense when attaching your dog to you by his leash; if your dog is large and out of control, it might not be safe to attach him to you. In that case, hold the leash in your hand, but try to avoid pulling on the leash to get him to pay attention and walk beside you.

*A length of soft nylon rope, a clasp, and duct tape are all that are needed to make a custom-length training leash.*

1.  If possible, start this exercise indoors where there will be few distractions and your dog can focus on his body movement. Work through the first six steps of this exercise before moving your training outside. Start close to a wall, a piece of furniture, or some other significant barrier that will force your dog to walk in a straight line when he is beside you. A hallway is a particularly good area to use for your initial training sessions. Have several small, tasty treats available. Attach your dog's leash to him and stand near the barrier or wall, facing your dog, with the leash around your waist or looped through a belt loop so you don't have to hold it in your hand. Quietly back away from him, offering him a small treat and plenty of praise after each step. Your dog should come in very close to you to get his treat; if you have to reach out to feed him, he is too far away and will have difficulty with the next training step. If he doesn't want to walk toward you as you back away, don't pull on the leash to get him to follow you. Instead, use a more valuable reward to motivate your dog to

move with you. Back away eight to ten steps, feeding after each step, then release him with your release cue. Do five repetitions of backing away per training session.

*Be sure to feed your dog close to you so he will be in the correct position for the second training step in this exercise. Gabriel has already worked through the first several steps of this exercise indoors and is now ready for training outdoors.*

2.  Once your dog immediately starts following you as you back away from him, you are ready to begin teaching him to walk in a straight line beside you. However, before actually working with your dog, practice your movements without him a few times to be sure you know exactly how you need to move.

    a.  Begin by backing away from your imaginary dog three or four steps, feeding him a small treat after every step. Take another step backward and pivot 180 degrees, so you and your dog end up facing the same direction. Take one step forward and feed your dog at your side. The direction you pivot is determined by which side you walk your dog on. If you pivot 180 degrees to your right, your dog will end up on your left side; if you pivot 180 degrees to your left, your dog will end up on your right side. You need to execute this move seamlessly so your dog does not stop moving. You are the one who will change direction. You back up, pivot, then walk forward; your dog simply walks in a straight line, in the same direction, the entire time.

*You are the one who changes direction; your dog continues walking forward in a straight line.*

b. Before actually walking with your dog, you will also need to figure out how close you need to be to the barrier when you pivot so you end up with your dog between you and the barrier. Your dog should have little extra room between you and the barrier; this will keep your dog from swinging wide or trying to circle around you while you walk and will help build his muscle memory for walking in a straight line beside you.

c. The last thing to work through before trying this with your dog is figuring out which hand you need to use to hold your treats. You should deliver treats out of the hand that is next to your dog when you are walking forward together. Because you don't have to hold the leash, your hands are free to hold and offer treats from either hand as you move. It doesn't matter if you prefer to have your dog walk on your right side or left side. Just be sure you feed him from the hand on the same side to prevent him from trying to reach across your body or circling in front of you to get his treat as you deliver it. If your dog walks on your left side, deliver treats from your left hand; if he walks on your right side, deliver the treats from your right hand. You want him to stay in position beside you while you deliver his treat. Slide your hand down your pant seam when you deliver it to help you resist the urge to reach out and reward him if he isn't right beside you. Remember, *where* you reward your dog plays an important part in helping your dog understand the behavior you want, so be sure to only reward your dog when he is close beside you. Using your real (or imagined) pant seam will help you be consistent with where you deliver your dog's reward and will give him a landmark to focus on when he is trying to learn where he is expected to walk. If you let him circle in front of you before you give him his treat, you are actually teaching him to get in front of you every time you stop, and are also unintentionally reinforcing the circling behavior you are trying to eliminate.

*Even if you are not wearing long pants, imagine sliding your hand down your pant seam when you are giving your dog his treat, to keep him in position beside you.*

d. Once you have your mechanics down, you are ready to try this with your dog. Put your dog on leash and start backing up, feeding after every step for three or four steps. Then pivot, take one step forward, reward your dog at your pant seam before he has the chance to move out of position, and release him with your release cue. If your dog moves ahead of you before you can give him his treat, withhold his reward; just because you have a treat in your hand does not mean you must give it to your dog if he is not close beside you. Instead, immediately start walking backward until your dog catches up to you again, then pivot and take a step forward and reward him along your pant seam before he has the chance to move out of position. Do not pull on the leash or nag him to get him back into position. Use your body language, the direction of your motion, and the appropriate delivery of rewards to teach your dog exactly where you expect him to walk. Do not use a verbal cue for this walking behavior yet; your dog does not really understand what you want yet and will still make mistakes that you do not want included in the final behavior. Let your motion and where you deliver his rewards show your dog what you want right now. You can certainly praise and talk to him while you train this behavior, but do not say "Heel" or any other cue yet. You will add a verbal cue when your dog is ready to start training outside. Make sure you do use your release cue after you take a step or two forward with your dog and reward him to let him know he is free to leave your side. After you reward and release him, set him up for another repetition. Complete five repetitions per training session.

3. As your dog gets more comfortable walking beside you, gradually increase your number of steps you take moving forward with him before rewarding and releasing him. Remember to be consistent in rewarding him along the seam of your pant leg so he gets his reward only when he is at your side. Use the 80% rule from Chapter 5 to decide when your dog is ready to walk a few more steps forward with you before you reward and release him. Training in sets of five makes the math easy—four out of five times equals 80%. Remain close to the barrier for this exercise step to continue to build his muscle memory for walking in a straight line. To help your dog stay focused on you, continue to start each repetition by backing up a few steps, feeding after each step, and then pivoting. If your dog gets out in front of you at any point, immediately start backing up, get his attention back on you, and then try moving forward again.

4. When your dog can walk for a dozen steps beside you without getting ahead of you, you are ready to increase the distance between your dog and the barrier. Back up a few steps, feeding after each one as you did before, but now execute your pivot about twelve inches farther away from the barrier than you did in the previous step, so the distance between your dog and the barrier is greater. If your dog starts to wander out of position laterally from you, adjust the distance between your dog and the barrier until he straightens out and walks close to you again. Make sure you continue to reward your dog along the seam of your pant leg so he stays close to you. As long as your dog moves in a straight line, you can gradually continue to increase the distance between the barrier and your dog over several training sessions. Reward and release him with your release cue before allowing him to move out of position. Do five repetitions per training session and apply the 80% rule to help you decide when you can move even farther away from the barrier.

5. When your dog can walk in a straight line beside you for a dozen steps with the barrier at least two feet away, you are finally ready to add a verbal cue to this new straight-line walking behavior. Back away a few steps to get your dog's attention on you, then give your verbal cue for straight-line

walking as you pivot to move forward with your dog; at that precise moment, your dog should be in perfect position at your side and should be able to maintain that position for several steps. If he isn't able to do that, wait to add the verbal cue until he can. This cue should be distinct from the cue you previously used when you took him out for walks on leash. You don't want to attach all the previous unacceptable walking behaviors to the new walking cue. If he is a herder or puller already, it will take time for him to learn his new walking behavior. But while you are teaching your dog how to walk nicely beside you, you still need to get him out for exercise. To avoid confusion, continue to use your original walking cue (the one you used before you started training this exercise) when you go out for your exercise walks, and use your new straight-line walking cue only when you are actually training him. This distinction between cues will help keep your new cue, and your dog's new straight-line walking behavior, strong. You will gradually get rid of your old cue when you start Step 8 of this exercise.

6. Your dog is now ready to start training outside. Start over with Step 4, using a curb, retaining wall, or similar raised barrier to continue to help him understand he can, and should, walk in a reasonably straight line next to you, even when you two are outside. Be sure your leash is securely attached to you, but if possible, don't hold it with your hands. You don't want to use the leash to control his motion. Instead, you want to teach him to control himself when you are out together. Use common sense when deciding where to start your outdoor training; do not risk being pulled down if your dog gets too excited while you have him attached to your waist. Pick calm locations to start your outdoor training and keep your training sessions very short. When you are using your old walking cue to exercise your dog, take the leash from around your waist and hold it safely until your dog learns to walk politely with you.

*Continue to use a barrier when you first start working your dog outside to help him maintain his straight-line walking behavior.*

7. When your dog can walk in a straight line beside you for about a dozen steps along outdoor physical barriers, you can gradually eliminate them. Start training on a sidewalk or path that has an obvious edge your dog can see. Now the barrier is visual instead of physical; your dog can easily wander off the cement and onto the grass if he circles or moves away from you, so be sure to pay attention to him while you walk. If you have slowly and methodically worked through all the previous steps, your dog has started to build muscle memory for walking in a straight line at your side and it should be reasonably easy for him to continue to do so on the sidewalk. If he wanders off the sidewalk, or tries to circle you, immediately start backing away from him to get his attention back on you, then pivot and move forward again. Don't forget to release him before he is allowed to move away from you. Start substituting environmental rewards for treats so you don't have to carry food with you every time you take your dog for a walk. For example, after your dog has walked politely

with you, you can praise him and release him to go read his pee-mail or sniff the grass as his reward for listening to you.

8.  To teach your dog to stay beside you for your entire walk, you must gradually increase the distance he walks in a straight line at your side. As you take your dog on his daily walks, start with one set of a dozen steps of straight-line walking per block. Use your old walking cue to fill in the gaps between sets of the new cue so you can continue to get in the distance necessary to give your dog some exercise while he is learning to walk in a straight-line for longer distances. This training takes time; don't expect your dog to be able to walk politely at your side for your entire walk as soon as you start training him outdoors. As his fluency continues to improve and he starts to understand he has to walk in a straight line on a loose leash no matter where you are, gradually increase the number of sets of a dozen steps you do per block, until your dog is able to walk an entire block in the correct position at your side. Then begin to increase the distance, one block at a time, until he is able to walk beside you without pulling or herding you for your entire walk. Just to be safe, particularly if your dog is one of the larger herding breeds, you can start holding the leash in your hand for added security in the event that your dog gets too excited while you are out and about. But don't fall back into the habit of tugging on the leash to control your dog; at this point, you shouldn't need to do that anyway.

9.  Finally, add in increasingly difficult distractions for your dog to manage while he is walking. If you respect your dog's bubble when you are out, he should be able to maintain a loose leash while walking at your side in most situations. But if something does burst his bubble, keep calm and move on! Over time, your dog will become more and more comfortable walking at your side, even when distractions are around.

Teaching your herding dog to walk in a straight line beside you takes time, effort, and patience. By giving your dog a definite position to assume while you are walking, you will help him better understand what you expect, and walks will become more pleasant for both of you!

## You talkin' to me?

**Exercise Goal:** Your herding dog will look toward you when you say his name.

Your dog's name is often the first thing you say when you want your dog to do something. It is easy to overuse or misuse your dog's name, without even realizing what you are doing. How many times a day do you say your dog's name? How many times do you say it for no particular reason? How many times do you pair his name with some type of correction? "Lassie, no!" "Lassie, get off that!" "Bad dog, Lassie!" If you aren't careful about the association you create for your dog when you say his name, your dog may begin to tune out his name as useless white noise or, worse yet, link his name with an imminent correction and actively start to avoid you whenever he hears it. However, if your dog associates his name with positive things, you will always have a handy way to quickly gain his attention when you need it, simply by saying his name.

1.  This exercise can be practiced any time, any place and you can use any type of reward with this exercise. Provide a different type of reward each training session to keep your herding dog guessing what fun will follow his name. Start this exercise with your dog on leash so he can't walk away from you. Say your dog's name once in a pleasant tone, and immediately give him a reward. Repeat five times per session and try to do several sessions each day. It doesn't matter if he doesn't look at you when you say his name for the first few times you go through this exercise; reward him anyway. You are simply trying to build an association in your dog's mind between hearing his name and receiving a reward.

2.  As your training progresses, you will notice that your dog will start to turn toward you as soon as he hears his name, anticipating a reward. When he is looking at you immediately after hearing his name at least 80% of the time (four out five repetitions), you can begin to pair his name with another cue he knows, such as "Sit" or "Down." Immediately follow the second cue with a reward and your release cue. Keep the behavior you want quick and easy to perform. Grabbing your dog's attention by saying his name before you cue him to perform any behavior will help him focus more on the behavior he is supposed to perform.

3.  Once your dog has a positive association with his name, you can also use it as an emergency backup recall for your dog. Take him out for a walk on a long line or a thin rope with a clasp tied to the end, so he can move a little distance away from you, without being able to run away. Let him get distracted enough to look away from you, then call his name once and immediately start moving toward something, as if you are hunting. Don't repeat his name or tell him to come; just start quietly "hunting." Run to a tree and look up in the branches, dig around in a patch of weeds, or look under a rock. Act as if whatever you are looking at is the most interesting thing that ever existed and ignore your dog (he's on his long line, so you know he can't run away). When your dog hears his name and turns toward you, he will see you engaging in an interesting behavior. If you are doing a good job of enjoying your special "hunt," he will probably come to you to join in the fun, even though you didn't ask him to come. Praise him profusely and reward him by allowing him to check out the place where you were looking before continuing your walk. Every once in a while make things extra exciting by dropping his favorite toy or a small treat where you are hunting so he can find it when he comes over to investigate.

Your dog should associate his name with pleasant interactions with you. Think like a dog and strengthen that association by hunting together. This teaches your dog that paying attention to you and being around you is fun, even when you are outdoors, and that his name means something good is going to come from you.

## Free ain't free

**Exercise Goal:** Your herding dog will remain near you until released, even after his leash is removed.

Many dogs who behave well when they are attached to a leash completely tune out their owners as soon as the leash is removed. For those dogs, removing the leash has become a cue that lets them know they are no longer under anyone's direct physical control. Off they charge as soon as the leash comes off, totally disconnected from their owners. Some herding dogs immediately start spinning, barking, or running circles around their owners as soon as they are free. Teach your dog to calmly hang around you after you take off his leash and leave you only after you give him permission to do so by giving him your release cue. This is a good safety behavior for him to learn. If his collar suddenly slips off or his leash ever breaks, you will have a reasonable chance of getting ahold of him if he knows it is worth his while to stay with you until you release him to leave.

This is an exercise that should be worked on every time you take the leash off your dog. Your dog is learning something every time you interact with him, so be sure he is learning to hang around you whenever you take his leash off until you give him your release cue, even if you aren't ending a formal training session.

1. For this exercise, you will need a lightweight leash in addition to his regular leash. Attach both leashes to your dog at the same time so he doesn't realize there is something extra hooked to his collar, and hold both leashes in the same hand as you go for your walk or have your training session. Have several small, tasty treats available.

*Ken has two leashes on his Belgian Tervuren Cali and is ready to start teaching her to stay near him after her leash is removed.*

2. At the end of your walk or training session, before removing the regular leash from your dog's collar, click the clasp without actually removing the leash and then immediately offer your dog a treat. Remain silent while you do this; the sound of the clasp clicking is going to become a cue to your dog to turn toward you in anticipation of a treat, instead of a cue that he is free to run off. Click the clasp and treat two or three more times without removing either leash. Now click the clasp on the regular leash and actually take it off your dog, leaving the lightweight leash on him. If your dog stays with you after you remove his regular leash, praise him and give him a treat; if he tries to take off when he feels the weight of the regular leash removed from his neck, be quiet. The lightweight leash will prevent him from leaving. This will likely surprise him. Step away from him as if nothing happened and reward him as soon as he catches up to you. Put his regular leash back on him while he is eating his treat, walk a few steps with him, and repeat. Don't cue him to sit or stay while you do this. In this exercise all your dog must do is stay by you until you give him his release cue. Let him figure out on his own that staying close to you, even after his leash is removed, earns him a reward. He must exhibit self-control to gain his freedom. When you have finished four or five repetitions, remove his regular leash, reward him for staying close

to you, remove the lightweight leash when you give him his release cue, and quietly walk away. His reward for the final repetition will be to go do whatever he wants to do.

3. Repeat this exercise every time you take the leash off your dog. Before long, you will notice that as soon as he hears his leash clasp click, he turns toward you. When at least 80% of the time he is remaining with you until you give him your release cue after you remove his regular leash, you can eliminate the second leash and start to add in other types of rewards (instead of treats) for staying near you after his leash is removed. Most of the time his reward can simply be praise and being released to do whatever he wants. But every once in a while, give him a treat, let him outside, or grab a toy and start playing with him after you remove the leash. Keep him guessing when and if you will give him a really special reward and he will be more willing to hang around with you after you take the leash off, just to see what's going to happen.

Consistency is very important in this exercise. Practice every time you take the leash off your dog, whether or not you are having a formal training session with him. Over time, you will become far more important than the leash when it comes to keeping your dog with you.

Owning a dog with a no-nonsense attitude toward anything he considers work, an urge to take control of anything moving, and a relatively low frustration threshold can be quite challenging. Learning basic management techniques to keep your dog out of frustrating situations in the first place and teaching him various ways to exhibit self-control are both very important to providing your herding dog appropriate behavioral boundaries and acceptable ways to cope with the challenges of modern urban life.

# Chapter 8

# Management and Training for Tenacity, Focus, and Obsessiveness

---

*A highly bred working dog [such as a herding dog] raised in a nonworking household environment will still show the working behaviors it has been selected to display, but it will display them abnormally. Worse, it will display those behaviors in bizarre and obnoxious ways.*

*Raymond Coppinger*
*Dogs: A New Understanding of Canine Origin, Behavior, and Evolution*

Herding livestock is mentally challenging, physically demanding, unpredictable, and dangerous work for both people and dogs. Herding has never been a job that can be left half done or finished tomorrow; no matter how long it takes, or what the cost, the job must be completed for the welfare of the livestock. Stories abound of herding dogs standing guard in blizzards over sheep that strayed from the flock, or collapsing from exhaustion after seeing the herd to safety over miles of treacherous terrain. Tenacity and focus, sometimes to the point of obsession, are traits that were selected for in herding dogs, out of work necessity. And those very same traits still exist to some extent in the herding dog you brought home, whether or not they are necessary for the lifestyle he leads with your family. There are several management techniques and training exercises in this chapter that you can use to help your herding dog overcome his natural tendency to get locked into his herding behaviors, while, at the same time, continuing to build his trust and confidence in you.

## Management techniques

### Games *not* to play with your herding dog

Your dog is learning something about his relationship with you every time you interact with him. Play is a powerful tool that can be used to encourage acceptable behaviors, as well as a destructive tool that can strengthen unacceptable behaviors. Many times the unacceptable behaviors your dog develops are enhanced by the games you play with him. Dogs don't do well with exceptions to the rules. If it is unacceptable to chase toddlers around the yard and nip at them, then it is equally unacceptable to chase teenagers around the yard and nip them, even though the teens are simply playing a game of keep-away from the dog. People should never be chased, regardless of size or age, in any context. Any game that encourages your herding dog to chase, bite, or bark at another person or animal should be avoided. There are many other ways your herding dog can express his herding instincts; he can herd his toys, chase after a ball, or even learn how to herd real livestock. But games that involve herding "sheeple" should never be allowed. One reason many herding dogs end up abandoned in shelters is that they bite someone or seriously injure or kill another dog or a cat. Often this happens in a split second of instinctive predatory behavior. Do not increase the odds that your herding dog will bite someone someday by playing risky chase-and-nip games with him that involve people or other animals.

Don't play games that involve having him chase things he can never catch, either. Herding dogs can be quirky. Shetland Sheepdogs sometimes engage in mindless tail-chasing behaviors. Several herding breeds, including Border Collies, are somewhat infamous for developing obsessive-compulsive chasing behaviors related to shadows, lights, or other visual stimuli, such as laser pointer dots. While it might be quite amusing to watch your dog try to catch a laser pointer dot, this type of game can bring out very destructive and harmful behaviors in your dog. If your dog becomes frustrated with the lack of anything he can interact with, or if he starts to generalize this chase behavior to other things he can't ever catch, like shadows or rays of light coming through a window, he can become nearly incapable of ignoring this type of stimulus, and very difficult to live with. Be fair with all games you play with your dog. If a chase game has no way for your dog to physically interact with the object of the chase, you shouldn't play that game with him.

*Herding a ball is a far safer game for German Shepherd Shishka to play than herding children or small animals.*

## If in doubt, don't!

Have you ever heard that little voice in your head that says "I'm really not sure this is going to end well…" when you are trying to decide if you should do something? That is the voice of common sense and it is an important one to listen to when you are trying to decide whether or not to do something with your dog. If you use common sense and always err on the side of caution in situations where you are not reasonably confident your dog will behave appropriately, you will never have to deal with regret (or worse) when something goes wrong. Because the question is never *if* something will go wrong, but *when* something will go wrong. Herding dogs are no-nonsense, intelligent, take-charge dogs. If you put your herding dog in a situation that he is not prepared to handle appropriately, the results could be disastrous. If you haven't taught your dog to calmly pass by a strange dog who is pulling wildly at the end of his leash, don't expect the situation to be fine if you throw caution to the wind and force your dog to share the sidewalk with an out-of-control dog. Your herding dog is apt to try to stop the erratic motion of the other dog, and that could lead to an unpleasant confrontation for both the dogs and their humans! If your dog hasn't learned to maintain control around running, screaming children, don't toss him in the backyard when your young child has friends over to play and hope for the best. You will likely end up with a nipped rear end or two when your dog tries to herd the children into a tidy flock, and an irate call from some child's parent because your dog "attacked" her child. If you haven't thoroughly trained your dog to handle situations that excite him, don't put him in those situations. It rarely works out well in the end.

## When to seek help for abnormal behaviors

Abnormal behaviors such as fly snapping, constant circling, shadow chasing, hypersensitivity to environmental stimuli, and self-mutilation can occur in herding breeds, especially in dogs who don't have some type of regular task to perform that utilizes their herding instincts. These behaviors can incapacitate a dog and require more than basic obedience training to change. If you own a herding dog, you *must* provide him routine, structured activity to keep him mentally healthy. If despite doing that your dog performs repetitive behaviors or appears to be a potential danger to himself, other dogs, or people, seek competent veterinary advice. Have physical reasons for his behavior, such as vision loss, hip dysplasia, or thyroid abnormalities, ruled out through a thorough physical exam.

If there are no obvious physical causes for your dog's extreme behavior, the next step is to consult with a board-certified veterinary behaviorist to determine if your dog's behavior requires medication, in addition to training, to modify. Psychopharmaceutical interventions are sometimes appropriate and necessary before any actual behavioral modification or training protocols can successfully alter these types of behaviors. The American College of Veterinary Behaviorists, listed in the Resources section at the end of this book, can help you locate a board-certified veterinary behaviorist in your area. These veterinarians have advanced training in cognition and behavior and understand the relationship between disease, medical intervention, and behavioral modification. They can help you determine if your dog's behavior can be altered through training and behavioral modification alone or if your dog would benefit from psychopharmaceutical intervention to help modify his abnormal behaviors. Many can also refer you to a certified canine behavioral consultant or canine behaviorist who can help you develop and implement a behavioral modification plan for your dog. Behavioral consultants and behaviorists primarily focus on reducing or eliminating unacceptable behaviors that are triggered by instincts or emotions, whereas trainers focus on teaching learned, acceptable behaviors. Be sure your behaviorist is certified by a reputable, independent credentialing program that requires proof of experience, knowledge, expertise, and continuing education. Your veterinary behaviorist and your canine behaviorist should be willing to work cooperatively (particularly if your dog is on medication) to create and implement a comprehensive treatment plan for your dog. It is far better to spend a few dollars on an appointment with a veterinary behaviorist only to find out that your dog's behavior can be altered by treating an underlying medical condition or through training alone, than to waste time and effort with training classes that will do nothing to change your dog's underlying mental and emotional conditions, if they are the source of his behavioral problems.

## Training exercises

The traits of tenacity, focus, and obsessiveness often show up when herding dogs encounter moving distractions. Without training, they may seem to lose all ability to listen and respond even to basic commands once they lock in on anything they think should be herded. Teaching your herding dog to focus on you and remain calm around moving distractions is critical to keeping your dog safe, particularly in urban settings.

## Attention target

**Exercise Goal:** Your herding dog will maintain eye contact with you on cue.

In her book *Collie Psychology*, Carol Price talks about the need to provide dogs with strong herding instincts an "obsession target" to focus on. This is an object, animal, or person that the dog can completely focus on while he is working. Dogs who actually herd can focus on the livestock. However, most herding dogs today never have the opportunity to work livestock. But they still have herding instincts and may still seek out something to focus those instincts on. If left to their own devices, they will select their own obsession targets, and more often than not, their choices will be inappropriate. Teaching your dog to focus on you as his obsession target will help you teach him to shift his focus away from distractions in his environment and pay attention to you instead. If your dog is looking at you, he can't also be fixated on the dog walking across the street, the car passing by, or the toy in the yard. You will get this focus from your dog by being more valuable to him than anything else, as discussed in Chapter 6, and by teaching him to give you eye contact on cue.

Keep in mind that in canine language, staring is rude and confrontational. Some dogs find it very stressful to break this canine social rule and give prolonged direct eye contact, while other dogs, especially Border Collies, who control livestock with their eyes, may find it difficult to stop staring. Be sure you keep a pleasant expression on your face and don't loom over your dog while you work through this exercise, and always use a release cue to let your dog know when the behavior is finished. Make sure you blink and breathe normally, too!

1. Start this exercise with your dog on leash in a quiet, calm environment. Have small, tasty treats available for rewards. Keep the treats in your pocket or in a bowl nearby so they won't distract your dog. If your dog isn't very motivated by treats, you can substitute a small toy. Sit or step on the end of the leash so you don't have to hold the leash and your dog can't decide to walk away while you are training.

2. Take one treat, show it to your dog, and slowly move it up to your face and hold it between your eyes. Don't say anything to your dog; let the treat do all the talking for you in this step. If the treat is one your dog really likes, he will naturally follow the treat up to your face and make eye contact with you in the course of tracking the treat. The moment his eyes meet yours, praise him, give him the treat, and release him. Yes, in this step, the attention is really all on the treat. Using a treat is a quick and easy way to teach your dog that it is okay to look you straight in the eyes. That is all you are trying to teach him at this point. Don't tell him to

watch yet; he doesn't really know what you expect him to do. For now let the treat do the talking for you. You will add the verbal cue later. Repeat five times per training session.

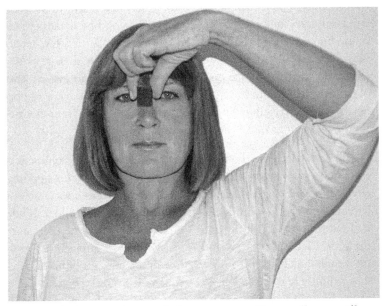

*Let the treat guide your dog's eyes to yours. Eventually you will not need the treat at your face to get eye contact from your dog.*

3.  To help your dog understand he can look at your eyes from any position he is in, practice having him look at your eyes when he is in different positions (sit, down, stand) and when he is in different positions relative to you (in front of you, beside you, at various angles to you). If you only train eye contact when your dog is sitting straight in front of you, he won't necessarily understand what you want when you cue him to give you eye contact when he is walking beside you or lying near you.

4.  Once your dog will immediately follow the treat up to your face and give you eye contact at least 80% of the time in a quiet environment, begin adding distractions to your training session. Don't worry about increasing the length of time your dog is watching you or moving the treat away from your eyes just yet. The first step in developing fluency will focus on ignoring environmental distractions for very short periods of time. Work up to at least 80% reliability around distractions that are moderately difficult for your dog before moving to the next step.

5.  When your dog understands how to make eye contact with you for short periods of time in distracting environments, it is time to work on getting rid of the treat stuck between your eyes as the cue for your dog to give you eye contact. Start this step in an environment with few distractions.

Quietly bring the treat up between your eyes as you did before, and then move it across your face, stopping with the treat next to your ear. Your herding dog will probably follow your hand as it moves; remain silent and wait for him to look back in your eyes. It may take a few moments, but he will eventually look back at you. The split second he makes eye contact, praise him, give him the treat, and release him. With a few repetitions, he will figure out that looking in your eyes, rather than at your hand, earns him the treat. Once he will quickly look at your eyes at least 80% of the time when you move your hand away from your eyes, add back the position and distraction work, as in Steps 3 and 4. Do five repetitions per training session to make the math calculation easy (4/5 = 80%).

6.  Continue to decrease the use of the treat as part of the physical cue for eye contact by making it less visible to your dog. Start this step in a quiet environment. Bring the treat up to your eyes, across to your ear, then let your wrist go limp and your hand drop to your shoulder. If your dog looks at your hand as it drops to your shoulder, resist the urge to say anything or wave the treat around to get your dog's attention. Simply wait for him to look back in your eyes, then praise him, give him the treat, and release him. He is on a leash, so he can't walk away. Be patient and quietly watch him try to figure out how to get the treat; he will eventually look at your eyes and you can praise him and give him the treat. When he will immediately look at your eyes at least 80% of the time even though you move your hand away, add back the position and distraction work, as in Steps 3 and 4. Do five repetitions per training session.

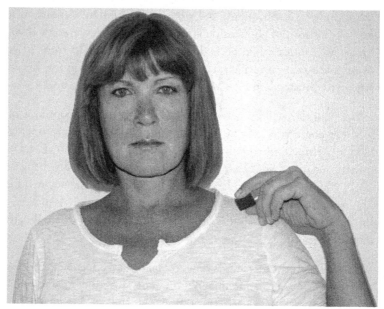

*Have patience while your dog figures out that he will get the treat if he looks at your eyes, instead of your hand.*

7. When your dog is 80% reliable giving you eye contact with your hand resting on your shoulder, it is time to get rid of the treat in your hand altogether and drop your arm to your side after giving your cue. For the first few training sessions, conceal the treats in your pocket, a treat bag, or a nearby bowl. Hold your hand as if you are holding a treat, then bring your hand up to your eyes, across to your ear, and down to your shoulder, then drop your arm to your side. Wait silently if your dog follows your hand with his eyes; this is a particularly difficult step for most dogs because now your hand is at or very near his eye level, making it harder to ignore. Be patient and quiet while he figures out he still needs to look at your eyes to earn his treat. As soon as he makes eye contact, praise him, reward him with a treat, and release him. Once he will quickly look at your eyes at least 80% of the time when you drop your arm to your side, add back the position and distraction work, as in Steps 3 and 4. Do five repetitions per training session.

8. You can now pair a verbal cue with your hand cue. Tell your dog "Watch" as you bring your hand up to your face. Because you have worked for many sessions to get your dog fluent with the behavior of giving you eye contact when you raise your hand toward your face, you can be reasonably confident he will actually be watching you when your give your verbal cue, even though he hasn't yet learned what your verbal cue means. By pairing the verbal cue with the hand cue, over time your dog will begin to associate the verbal cue with the behavior. You can also start using other types of rewards (praise alone, a toy, going outside) in place of treats when he gives you eye contact. Vary his reward so he never knows what he will earn by giving you his undivided attention.

9. One of the last components of eye contact to add in is duration. This is accomplished by simply delaying the delivery of the reward after your dog gives you eye contact. Instead of immediately giving him his reward after he gives you eye contact, you will start to wait before rewarding him. Be sure to increase the amount of time he must look at you to earn his reward in small increments so he can be successful. Increasing the duration by one- or two-second intervals will help you progress slowly but steadily toward your ultimate duration goal. Give him his release cue as soon as you reward him. If he stops looking at you before you release him, don't give him his reward. Instead, give him his release cue, then quickly set him up again and decrease the length of time he must give you eye contact before being rewarded and released, so he can be successful.

10. The last step in teaching your dog to give you stationary eye contact is to gradually add more distractions to his environment. When you increase the difficulty of the distraction, decrease how long you expect him to

watch you for the first few training sessions. You want a few quick successes with the more difficult distraction before you start increasing the duration again. Work on the edge of your dog's bubble for each distraction so he will be able to keep his focus on you when you ask for eye contact. Following the 80% rule, gradually decrease the distance between your dog and the distraction so he can be closer to distractions and still give you eye contact. As the distraction difficulty increases, so should the reward value. For example, if your dog gets really excited by cyclists and he gives you eye contact as a cyclist passes by, give him a jackpot of some of his favorite rewards to mark that exceptionally difficult behavior he just completed. This will keep your dog motivated to pay attention to you even when exciting distractions are around.

11. So far you have asked for your dog's attention only when he is stationary. There will be times you want or need your dog to give you attention for short periods of time while you are walking together (e.g., when you are passing a distraction). After he is fluent in giving you stationary eye contact, you can teach him how to give you attention while moving. Moving eye contact is more difficult for your dog to perform: first, you are asking him to trust that he won't walk into anything while he is looking at you; and second, he also has to figure out how to walk while maintaining eye contact with you. When you add motion to attention work, start with your dog standing beside you in a quiet environment where he is comfortable walking, such as an indoor hallway. Go back to holding a treat near your eyes for the first few sessions to help him understand where to look when he is moving. You may need to twist slightly toward your dog the first few training sessions so he can see your eyes and the treat in your hand more easily and figure out he can give you eye contact and walk at the same time. As soon as he is able to maintain eye contact with you for a few steps, straighten your body back into your natural walking position so he can learn how to find your eyes when you are standing upright, facing straight forward. Cue him with your hand and voice to look at you, and once you have eye contact, take one or two steps forward, praise him, reward him if he is still giving you eye contact, and release him. If he isn't still looking at you, withhold the reward and quietly try again. If your dog can't do two steps without breaking eye contact, try a single step. If he can't even do that, go back and work on the stationary attention for a few more sessions to be sure he really understands the basic concept of watching you. As your dog becomes more comfortable watching you while he is in motion, you can gradually increase the distance you move together the same way you increased duration in Step 9, and then increase the difficulty of the distractions he must ignore while giving you moving eye contact. The last step is to start working on this behavior outside.

*Being able to get your dog's attention while you are walking is helpful when you need to move past distractions on a walk.*

Teaching your herding dog to give you eye contact takes time, but once he understands how to pay attention to you on cue, you will be able to make more progress toward controlling other aspects of his behavior. Although it is not realistic to expect strict attention from your dog for the entire duration of a walk around the neighborhood, it is realistic to ask for a few steps of focused attention at random times during your walk to help you stay connected with one another, and to teach him to maintain eye contact with you while you walk past distractions together.

## Park it

**Exercise Goal:** Your herding dog will learn to go to and stay in a well-defined area.

This exercise will give your herding dog a job to focus on even when you don't actually want him to do anything. Being able to send your dog to a particular spot in a room while you eat supper or have him comfortably rest on a mat in the vet clinic lobby while you wait for the vet is very useful. Teaching your dog this exercise is also a component of teaching polite door greetings, explained in detail in Chapter 9.

A useful parking space for your dog is a rubber-backed bath mat. This type of mat will work on any surface without sliding and provides some cushioning for your dog while he is on it. It can easily be washed and is a practical size to take along when you go out with your dog to the vet clinic or training classes.

1. For this exercise, start in an area that has enough room for you to put down the mat and still have space around all four sides for your dog to walk. Have small, tasty treats ready that will be easy for your dog to see on the mat; if the mat is dark, use light-colored treats, and vice versa. Treats that don't easily roll are also useful so they will stay put on the mat when you toss them. Before you bring your dog out to work, practice tossing a few treats on the mat to perfect your aim and avoid adding unnecessary confusion to the training process through poorly tossed treats.

2. Your dog's parking space should be a place he associates with good experiences. To introduce him to the mat and the concept of getting good things while he is on it, start with your dog on leash, close enough to the mat that he has to take only one or two steps to get on it. Show your dog a treat and then toss it, aiming to get the treat to land on the far side of the mat. Your dog should move forward to get his treat when he sees you toss it. If he doesn't, point out the treat and encourage him to step on the mat to get it. As soon as your dog eats the treat you tossed, offer him another treat while he is still on the mat, and then quickly back away as you give him his release cue and encourage him to move off his mat. Repeat the toss five times per training session until your dog starts to move toward his mat as soon as he sees you move your arm to toss the treat. Don't give him any verbal cue for this behavior yet. Allow your arm motion and the treat to get your dog to go to his mat.

3. When, at least 80% of the time, your dog is starting to move toward the mat as you begin to toss the treat, take one step back from the mat and toss a treat. As he moves to his mat, quietly step toward the mat (if necessary) to feed him another treat when he is still on his mat, and then give him his release cue and allow him to leave his mat. Your dog doesn't have to sit or lie down at this point. He just needs to get all four feet on the mat to earn that second treat from you.

*Your arm motion is the cue for your dog to go to his mat to get his treat.*

4.  Continue to increase the distance between your dog and his mat one step at a time until you are too far away to toss a treat on the mat reliably. If you used the 80% rule to determine when to increase the distance between your dog and his mat, he should be anticipating getting a treat on his mat as soon as he sees you move your arm toward the mat in a tossing motion, even if you don't actually toss a treat. Pretend to toss a treat to the mat using the same motion you used when you were standing closer. Your dog should immediately move to his mat, expecting a treat to be there. Follow behind him quickly and quietly and hand him his treat as soon as he has all four feet on his mat. And don't forget to praise him, too! Give him his release cue and allow him to leave his mat.

Continue to increase the distance a step or two at a time until you can send him from one side of the room to the other to get on his mat. If he leaves his mat before you can walk over to give him his treat, take him back half the distance you just sent him, motion toward his mat to get him to go to it, step in behind him, and give him his treat before he has the chance to leave the mat. Take him back the full distance for the next repetition; if he leaves the mat early again, he may not be ready for you to send him from that far away. Use the 80% rule to determine when your dog is ready for you to increase the distance to avoid unnecessary confusion and frustration for your dog. If your dog is going all the way to his mat at least 80% of the time on a single cue, you can also add in a verbal "Park it" cue as you move your hand. As your dog begins to understand his job better and associates the verbal cue with going to his mat, you can start to decrease the amount of arm motion you use to get him to go to his mat. Eventually, he will be able to go to his mat on his verbal cue alone or by you simply pointing toward his mat.

5.  Now is a good time to decide where you would like to position your dog's parking space in any given room. It will be easier for your dog to go to his mat consistently if he knows exactly where to expect his mat to be in each room. For example, if you would like your dog to go to his mat in the kitchen so he isn't under your feet while you prepare dinner, select an out-of-the-way spot in the kitchen where he can see you, but not interfere with you, and put his mat there. If you want to use mats in several rooms in your house, buy several mats and be sure to practice this exercise in each room so he learns where to look for his mat.

6.  The first five steps of this exercise focused only on getting your dog to *go* to his mat. Now it's time to teach him to *stay* on it. In order for this to be a truly useful behavior to teach your dog, he needs to know that he may be expected to spend some time on his mat. Send your dog to his mat and follow quietly behind him. Once he is on his mat, treat him, but delay giving him his release cue for a few seconds. If you taught him his release cue, he already knows he should continue doing whatever you've cued him to do until you release him, so he should stay on the mat. If he leaves, simply direct him back onto his mat, but don't wait quite so long this time before you release him, so he has success remaining on his mat. Use the 80% rule to increase the time you wait, in short increments of one to five seconds, before you release your dog to leave his mat. Be sure to stay close to your dog while he is learning to stay on his mat for longer periods of time. Because most herding dogs are exceptionally sensitive to anything in their personal space, quietly stepping in front of him to block his path as he tries to leave his mat will likely cause him to move back onto it. Be sure to praise him as soon as all four feet are back on the mat

to emphasize you want him to stay on it. Ideally, he should never get all four feet off the mat before you help him get back on; the quicker you direct him back on to his mat, the sooner he will learn to stay on it until he is released. You may notice your dog changes position on his mat as he is expected to remain there longer. That's okay! You did not cue him to sit or lie down; you cued him to go to his mat and stay on it. As long as he doesn't leave his mat, he is free to adjust himself and get comfortable in any way he desires.

7.  Once your dog has worked up to a minute or so staying on his mat, you need to start increasing the distance that *you* remain from him when he is on it. There is no point teaching your dog to go to his mat in the kitchen and stay there if you have to go over to his mat and stay with him every time you send him there. By now, your dog knows how to travel across the room to get to his mat and stay there for short periods of time, but he is used to you following behind while he does this. He needs to learn how to go to his mat without you following him. Drop a treat on the mat and take your dog about halfway across the room. Cue him to go to his mat and take one small step toward it as if you are going to follow him, then slowly come to a stop. Chances are good that he will continue on to his mat. If he does, he will be immediately rewarded with the treat you left on the mat. If he stops moving when you stop moving, quietly step closer to his mat until he starts moving again. On the next repetition, walk behind him for a few more steps before stopping so your dog will successfully go straight to his mat in one motion. Be very calm and slow with your body language if your dog struggles with moving ahead of you to go to his mat; be quiet and let him figure out he can go there by himself. Gradually increase the distance he has to go out in front of you to get to his mat by a step or two at a time, until you can stay on one side of the room and send him to his mat on the other side without you following him. Leave a treat on the mat before you take him across the room to send him, so he is immediately rewarded for the correct behavior. Once he is on his mat, be sure he doesn't leave until you give him his release cue. Keep your eye on him and be ready to step in to help him stay on his mat if he tries to leave, as you did in the previous steps.

8.  When your dog is promptly going to his mat by himself and staying on it for a few minutes, you can introduce long-lasting rewards he can enjoy while he is on his mat. You can give him his meal, a chew toy stuffed with a tasty frozen filling, or his favorite non-food chew toy to enjoy on his mat and occupy his mind while he is waiting to be released. If he leaves his mat before you release him, or his reward rolls off the mat and he leaves to get it, pick up the reward and send him back to his mat before giving him the reward back. It is important to pay attention to your dog

while he is learning he must stay on his mat even when you are at a distance. The faster you get him back on his mat if he tries to leave it, the easier it will be for him to understand that leaving was the behavior that you didn't want him to do; ideally, if you keep an eye on him and slowly increase the distance between you and your dog, you will be able to help him get back on his mat before all four feet have left it. Keep the rewards you give him when he is on his mat extra valuable by giving them to him only when he is on his mat.

9. Distractions are the last thing to add into your mat work. The distractions you need to work around will depend on how you will use this behavior in everyday life. Now that your dog knows how to go to his mat from across the room and stay there until you tell him he can leave, you can use his parking space as a place to hang out while you prepare dinner or as his own personal space to occupy when you go to training class. If you want to use the mat in the kitchen, you need to introduce the sights, sounds, and smells of food preparation to your dog while he stays on his mat. Feeding him his meal on his mat while you are cooking will help him have patience and remain in place. If at any time he leaves his mat without being released, you need to put him back on it immediately. If you are preparing a gourmet multi-course meal and don't have time to work with potential training issues that may pop up, don't put your dog on his mat in the first place. Use alternative ways to keep him out of the kitchen and out of your way. If you want to use his mat in training class, place it next to your chair and be sure to keep an eye on him while other students are working or the instructor is talking. If he leaves his mat, put him right back on it so he understands the same rules that apply to his mat behavior at home also apply in class. You may want to give him his favorite binkie toy to chomp on if he is extremely nervous or frustrated with idle time in class, or if he isn't particularly food-motivated to begin with; he may get aroused to the point that he refuses food in class but will still shake, chew, or otherwise take his frustrations out on a toy while he remains on his mat.

Park It is a useful behavior on its own, but is also an important component of many other behaviors. Chapter 9 details one of many different advanced mat behaviors you can teach your dog, which involves going to his mat when he hears the doorbell ring to help control inappropriate door behaviors like spinning, barking, and jumping on people.

*Gabriel lies on his mat and chews on his binkie toy while
he waits his turn to work in an outdoor training class.*

## Stay means stay

**Exercise Goal:** Your herding dog will maintain a stationary position around people
and moving objects.

Motion is one thing most herding dogs find very difficult to ignore. Sometimes they
confuse a bicycle moving down the sidewalk with a sheep bolting from the flock, or
a child running around in the yard with an errant calf, and their instinctual herding
behaviors kick into high gear. The dog may bark, chase, and quite possibly bite at
whatever is moving. These situations can be very problematic and potentially dangerous for all involved. Teaching your herding dog to remain stationary while people and
objects move around him is a critical skill for him to master, particularly if you live in
a busy urban area. Combine this exercise with the Stop and Drop and Moving Stop
and Drop exercises in Chapter 7 for the best safety behavior for your dog.

1. Before you start working with your dog, you need to collect some information. First, you will need to figure out exactly which moving objects
   trigger your dog's herding instincts. You also need to identify the size of

his bubble for each object, so you know how far away you need to be from each to begin your training; work through Respect the Bubble in Chapter 7, if you haven't already done so, before starting this exercise. You should also determine how much motion is necessary to get your dog excited. If your dog has a long history of chasing moving objects, like bicycles and cars, those objects may trigger a herding response even when they are not moving. Also, figure out if sounds affect your dog's response to motion. Some dogs can ignore objects that move quietly, but react strongly to noisy ones, like motorcycles, vacuum cleaners, or screaming children. Finally, decide which position (sit, down, or stand) you are going to cue your dog to assume while an object moves by. This may seem like quite a bit of information to gather simply to teach your dog to stay, but it will help you tailor your dog's training specifically to his needs and save you wasted time and effort.

2. Start this exercise with your dog on leash and have a generous supply of small, tasty treats accessible. Select a moving object that causes you and your dog problems on a routine basis and start with that object in a stationary position. For example, if your dog chases and tries to nip cyclists, start with a bicycle leaning on its kickstand or against a wall. Bring your dog as near to the bike as you can without him losing his ability to pay attention to you. Cue him to assume the position you are going to cue him to hold when cyclists pass by. Give him a single cue, wait a second or two for him to respond, and if he doesn't perform the behavior, gently help him into the correct position. If you have to help him, immediately give him his release cue, allow him to get up, and then move farther away from the bike before you cue him to sit again. You want your dog to be successful holding his position, so you may need to adjust the distance between him and the bike to accomplish that goal. If you remain too close to the bike, your dog will continue to get more aroused as his focus on the bike intensifies, making it more difficult for him to respond to any cue you give him. If your dog performs the behavior but refuses his treat, increase your distance as well. Loss of appetite can be an indicator of arousal; the more excited a dog gets around an object, the less interested he is in eating and the more focused he may become on interacting with whatever has his attention. Make sure you are using exceptionally tasty treats for this exercise. Even if your dog typically chases bicycles in motion, be prepared for him to react to the mere sight of one, and set him up for success right from the start.

3. Once you assess how close you can be to the stationary bicycle, ask your dog for a few quick repetitions of the position you want him to assume. If you decide to use a sit for this behavior, do a few quick sits, reward him while he is sitting, and then release him immediately. Gradually delay the reward and release cue, requiring him to hold the sit for longer periods of

time before he is rewarded and released. Vary how long you ask your dog to hold his position, so he can't predict when he will get his release cue. For example, if you are doing five repetitions of this exercise in a training session, the first sit might be immediately released, the second sit might have a delay of two seconds, the third sit might have a delay of three seconds, the fourth sit might be immediately released again, and the fifth sit might have a delay of one second. Even though the initial training sessions involve holding his position for very short periods of time, varying the length of time your dog has to hold his position will keep him from anticipating his release and will set your dog up for a better understanding of the behavior. Repeat five times per training session and use the 80% rule to decide when you can increase the length of time your dog has to hold his position.

*Gabriel requires four feet between him and the
bike to remain calm, sit on cue, and eat treats.*

4.  Before moving your dog closer to the bike, work your dog up to holding his position for fifteen seconds or more at a comfortable distance away. There is nothing magical about that amount of time, but you want your dog to be very solid remaining in his position before you start making the distraction more difficult for him by moving him closer to it. You can ask him to hold his position longer before you move him closer to the bike if you want, but don't move closer if he can't calmly hold his position at least fifteen seconds while he is working at a distance you have determined to be comfortable for him.

5. Decrease the distance between your dog and the bike one step at a time, until your dog can sit for fifteen seconds or more right beside the bike and remain calm and continue to listen to you. Your dog will make quicker progress if you decrease the distance in small increments over several training sessions than if you try to decrease the distance in a big increment and he fails repeatedly. If your dog can't remain in a sit for fifteen seconds when he is six feet away from the bike, it makes no sense to expect him to hold his position when he is six inches away. Being close to the bike and calmly sitting until he is released should lead to great rewards from you. If he breaks his sit, quickly and quietly help him sit in the spot where he had been sitting, so he doesn't end up closer or farther from the bicycle, then immediately release and repeat again, a little farther away, so he can be successful.

6. When your dog can successfully hold his position at least 80% of the time he is around the stationary bicycle, it is time to introduce motion. Always do this exercise with your dog on leash and securely under your control. If he is not leashed and breaks his position to chase the bike once it starts moving, he may hurt the rider or get hurt himself. Because a bicycle requires a rider to make it move, start this step with the rider seated on the bike, but not moving. Begin at the same distance from the bike you started at in Step 5, and gradually decrease the distance over the next few training sessions until he is comfortable sitting close to the stationary rider and bike. Increase the distance once again when you finally put the rider and bike in motion. Methodically work through Step 5 again with a slow-moving bike and later a fast-moving one, using the 80% rule to help you decide when your dog is ready for the bicycle to speed up. Your goal is to teach your dog to hold his position at a reasonable distance from a moving bike. He really only needs to learn to hold his position a few feet away from a moving bicycle, because your dog may end up that close to one if you step off a sidewalk or path to allow a cyclist to pass. With other moving objects, like cars, your dog needs to learn to hold his position at a distance you typically are from moving traffic when you walk your dog. No matter how well your dog is handling his stays around any moving object, always have your dog on leash and physically under your control when you are out in public with him, in case he breaks his position and tries to run after whatever is moving. Safety is your responsibility!

7. When your dog is able to sit calmly near a moving bike or whatever other moving object you're training with, you can ask him to give you eye contact while he is sitting. The Attention Target exercise earlier in this chapter will help you teach your dog to do this. If your dog is focusing on you, he can't also be focusing on the bike, car, etc., and become frustrated because he can't chase it.

Modern city life is full of quick-moving objects, living and mechanical. Any of them can become the focus of your dog's attention and trigger instinctive herding behaviors. Teaching your dog to remain stationary and calm enough to listen to you around such things is critical to helping him successfully cope with urban living.

## Stop the spin cycle

**Exercise Goal:** To provide your dog an alternative to spinning behaviors when he is excited.

When your herding dog frantically spins or runs tight circles around you, he is demonstrating displaced herding behaviors. This instinctive behavior occurs because he is very frustrated, is very excited, or has learned that spinning earns him attention from you. Spinning can interfere with his ability to pay attention to you and can become a chronic problem that prevents you from working as a team. You will need to work through this exercise with each object or situation that triggers spinning behavior, but only work with one trigger at a time during a training session so you don't overwhelm your dog.

1. Have your dog on leash and a really valuable reward ready to give him. This is not the time to be stingy or boring with his rewards! Put the exciting object that triggers spinning out of sight in the area you are going to train in, so your dog can remain calm to start this exercise. Your dog needs to be on leash in case you have to limit the spinning he may do while you are training. Skip to Step 6 if the object that triggers his spinning is the leash; if your voice and attention trigger spinning, skip to Step 9.

2. Slowly and matter-of-factly, bring out the object that excites your dog and set it down a few feet from your dog. Let him see the object, but don't make a big deal out of it. Simply let your dog look at it. You must remain quiet, calm, and relaxed while your dog works through this exercise. If your dog starts to spin, stand still and quietly wait for him to stop spinning, even if it is only momentarily. Don't contribute to his excitement by yelling at him or repeating commands to try to get him to stop. You need to let *him* figure out that spinning is not a behavior that will earn him the object or anything else he wants from you. He's already had practice with this behavior and it is a derivation of instinctive herding behavior, so it may take quite some time for him to figure this out. However, if you are quiet, consistent, and persistent with this exercise, you can significantly reduce, or eliminate, his spinning. If he is already so focused on the object that he can't stop spinning after fifteen seconds, gently move him farther away from the object until he can stop spinning.

3. When he stops spinning, no matter how briefly, praise him in a calm, slow voice and give him a really special reward. It does not matter what

behavior he does once he stops spinning; he simply needs to stop spinning. While he is enjoying his special reward, place the exciting object out of sight again so you are set up to do another repetition. Be careful to keep praise low-key but sincere, so you don't trigger spinning with your enthusiasm. If he starts spinning when you praise him, don't give him his special reward. Instead, wait again for him to stop spinning briefly. Then be very calm and soothing (and brief!) with your praise and quickly give him his reward before he starts spinning again. Do five repetitions per training session, then put the exciting object out of sight until the next training session.

4.  When your dog can look at the object without any spinning, you are ready to pick it up, if it is one you would normally handle (e.g., a toy you would pick up to throw). Simply pick it up and immediately set it back down. Be on your toes to quickly reward calm behavior from your dog. He might regress a little in his self-control when you start to move the exciting object; that's okay—just keep the experience as short and non-exciting as possible. Don't say anything or try to move the object closer to your dog while you pick it up. Keep the 80% rule in mind to help you gradually increase the length of time you interact with the object and the length of time your dog must resist the urge to spin in order to earn his reward.

5.  When your dog can tolerate you handling and holding the exciting object without breaking into a spin, you can start offering him the object itself (if you are working with an object you normally would give to him, like a toy) as his reward for remaining calm. You must also remain calm when you offer it to him. You do not want to trigger spinning by an overly dramatic presentation; sometimes dogs get crazy about an object simply because their owners get goofy whenever the object is around. Dogs take in everything that is going on in their environment, and if you are too excited around a particular object, chances are your dog will also eventually become too excited when he sees it and may start to spin. Calmly and quietly praise him and offer him the object as his reward if he doesn't spin. This object should be no more special than any other reward he receives as far as you are concerned. If he starts spinning before you actually give it to him, wait until he stops spinning to let him have it. Spinning should never lead to a reward for him.

6.  If the leash triggers spinning, you have a significant training challenge to overcome. While he is learning to remain calm when he sees his leash, you still need to take him out on leash for exercise! So how do you keep him from practicing his spinning behavior while he is learning how to remain calm when he sees his leash? By managing your dog's behavior while you are leashing him up to take him outside! Instead of taking the

leash to your dog, take your dog to the leash. Gently take your dog by his collar and lead him as close as possible to the door before putting his leash on. Keep ahold of him on a very short leash to prevent him from spinning until you actually get out the door. You are not teaching him not to spin with this handling; you are just preventing him from practicing the spinning behavior while he is learning how to remain calm when he sees his leash. If necessary, gently hold him by his collar when you open the door if you can't stop his spinning with a short leash, so he is physically calm as he is allowed to step outside. You must combine management with training to help your dog change his behavior when he sees his leash; it won't be perfect, but the more spinning you prevent, the easier it will be for your dog to break his spinning habit. If he starts spinning during your walk, stop and quietly wait for him to stop before moving on.

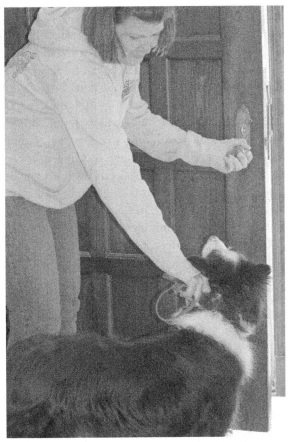

*Gently holding your dog by the collar will physically prevent him from spinning when you open the door; it is a useful management technique until he learns how to remain calm on his own.*

7. Leashes can be exciting because they are usually brought out immediately before your dog gets to do something fun with you, like take a walk or go for a ride in the car. Over time, your dog starts to anticipate these activities whenever he sees his leash. Add to the dog's anticipation the habit many owners have of talking excitedly and moving quickly when attaching the leash and it should be no surprise that many herding dogs lose self-control and start spinning at the mere sight of their leashes. Most dogs are leashed up near the door, so moving toward the door can also trigger spinning. The initial training space you use for leash work should be away from the door, preferably somewhere in your house where you don't normally leash up your dog. By starting this training in a different location, you will remove extra environmental cues that may be contributing to your dog's spinning behavior, making it easier for him to maintain self-control.

To actually teach your dog to remain calm when he sees his leash, start as you did in Step 2, using the leash as the exciting object. Work through Steps 2 through 5 until your dog can resist the urge to spin when you pick up the leash and attach it to his collar. Be sure you reward his stillness with other rewards he really values; don't be stingy! After attaching his leash and rewarding him for staying calm, quietly walk away and let him drag his leash around the house a bit without taking him out. Dogs notice patterns; putting a leash on was always followed by going outside and working with you in some manner. It is time to break that pattern if your dog continues to spin after you put his leash on. By allowing him to drag the leash around without taking him outside, you are starting to weaken the association between having his leash put on and immediately going outside. After a few minutes, if he is not spinning, quietly take his leash back off, reward him, and put the leash away. Train in different places in your house each training session and let him drag the leash around a bit before removing it, until he no longer spins after you put it on. Continue to use the management techniques described in Step 6 to get your dog outside for his daily on-leash exercise.

8. When your dog no longer spins after you put the leash on and let him drag it, you are ready to actually pick the leash up and hold it. Start this step away from the door. If your dog remains calm and doesn't spin, reward him, remove his leash, and release him. If he starts to spin, drop his leash and walk away until he stops spinning. Spinning should never lead to something your dog wants; only calm behavior will open the gate to good things from you. Gradually move your training sessions closer to the door as he learns to remain calm when you attach his leash and hold on to it. When your dog no longer spins when you are holding his leash, even when you are near the door, it is time to use going for a walk,

instead of treats, as his reward for being calm. If at any point your dog starts spinning before you get outside, turn around and move away from the door. Drop his leash and walk away until he stops spinning, then try to move outside again. Be careful not to contribute to your dog's excitement by making a big deal out of going outside. Just leash him up and move matter-of-factly toward the door. Praise him in low, slow, soothing tones for remaining calm. His reward for resisting the urge to spin is the walk you are going to take together. If he starts spinning while you are out for your walk, stop walking and stand quietly until your dog stops spinning. Pay attention to the distraction that triggered the spinning and work with that in future training sessions, if possible. He needs to remain calm from the time you take the leash out to put it on until the time you take it off and put it away. If you don't have time to actually do some training before leaving the house, use the management techniques in Step 6 to get out the door as quickly as possible.

9. If the mere sound of your voice or the sight of you causes your dog to spin out of control, do an honest assessment of your interactions with him. It is possible your dog is acting crazy around you because you are acting crazy around him! If you talk too excitedly or move too quickly, particularly when you first greet him after you've been away awhile, he may simply be mirroring your excitement by spinning. To determine if your behavior is the cause of your dog's spinning, simply greet your dog very calmly and quietly, and see what he does. He may automatically start to spin when he sees you, particularly if you have a long history of being crazy during greetings, but your calm behavior should quickly slow him down or stop his spinning altogether. If that is the case, you need to control your own behavior in order to effectively teach your dog to control his. Be calm and slow in your motions, and use a conversational tone of voice when you talk to him. Over time, he will start to mirror your calmness and the spinning will fade.

If your own calm behavior has absolutely no impact on your dog's behavior, then you need to ask yourself if you are giving your dog all the daily attention, physical exercise, and mental stimulation he requires to be truly healthy and happy. If all it takes to make your herding dog lose self-control is the mere sight of you, chances are very good that he needs *significantly more* attention from you on a regular basis than you are currently giving him. Herding dogs are very time-intensive, labor-intensive dogs to live with as pets. They are, first and foremost, highly specialized "tools" that require daily work of some sort to be behaviorally and physically healthy. These breeds weren't developed to be lap dogs or indoor pets who need relatively little physical or mental stimulation. You may be willing to tolerate prolonged, frantic spinning or other repetitive behaviors from your herding dog every time he sees you, but that means you are also forcing your dog to tolerate a life of frustration spinning in anticipation of doing something with you to alleviate his boredom and stress. The only way to impact his spinning behavior is by making the lifelong commitment to providing him the daily exercise and training he craves. As you begin to provide him adequate exercise and training, some of his spinning will naturally decrease as his frustration and anxiety decrease.

If you can't make that commitment, for whatever reason, then re-homing your dog with someone who will be able to fulfill his innate needs is a loving solution to the situation. There is no shame in recognizing that you can't give your dog what he needs and then making the effort to find someone who can provide those things to him; the shame comes in forcing him to live his life frustrated and anxious because you don't want to get rid of him, but can't, or won't, provide him what he needs to be healthy and happy. There are many breed-specific rescue groups that can help you find a loving home for your dog if you make the decision to re-home him. An Internet search will provide you plenty of contact information for these groups.

Don't expect significant changes in your dog's spinning behavior in just a few training sessions. It took time for him to develop the habit of spinning and it will take him time to learn the new habit of remaining calm. Be consistent and persistent, and your dog will learn there are more acceptable ways to express his frustration or excitement than by spinning himself silly!

# Chapter 9

# Management and Training for Barking

*A dog in his kennel barks at his fleas; a dog hunting doesn't notice them.*

*Chinese proverb*

It is difficult, if not outright impossible, to completely extinguish a dog's instinct to vocalize. Dogs naturally communicate with each other by barks, growls, whines, and howls. Trying to teach your dog never to vocalize is not realistic, nor is it kind. It is the canine equivalent of telling a person he can never talk, sing, yell, or laugh again as long as he lives. That would be an impossible feat for any human with normal vocalization capacities. Even monks who voluntarily take vows of silence are allowed to speak under a few very exceptional circumstances! Likewise, it is impossible for any dog with the ability to vocalize to never bark or whine. Barking is your dog's native language and it is a normal, healthy activity that will always be a part of his behavioral repertoire.

Certain herding breeds instinctively bark more than others do as they work. Sadly, the tendency of some of these breeds (e.g., Shetland Sheepdogs and Collies) to bark excessively when they are bored or stressed leads some owners to surgically de-bark their dogs as a quick fix to the noise. But de-barked dogs continue to vocalize; the resulting sounds are reduced to harsh, raspy "whispers" that can be just as irritating, although not quite as loud, as a normal bark. This radical procedure, which involves severing the vocal cords, causes unnecessary physical pain and does absolutely nothing to alter a dog's instinctive urge to bark, nor does it alleviate the underlying instinct or emotion that triggered the barking in the first place. Barking is a self-soothing behavior that some dogs engage in as a way to expend pent-up physical energy. Although excessive barking is definitely unacceptable in most situations, the goal of training should never be to extinguish barking altogether. The goal should be to limit barking to an acceptable level through management and training. It will take time and consistency to teach your dog to control his barking, but your entire neighborhood will thank you for your efforts!

## Management techniques

### Be quiet as a mouse

Have you ever been out on a walk with your dog and suddenly he stopped, cocked his head, and started rooting around in the grass looking for something? Your dog probably heard an insect or small animal moving through the grass and decided to investigate. Because they are predators, dogs are genetically hard wired to pay attention to faint, prey-like sounds. If your dog is not suffering from an actual physical hearing loss (and most aren't), talking to him at a conversational volume level is more than loud enough for him to hear you. Just because your dog does not respond to your cues doesn't mean he didn't hear them. There is probably another reason he didn't respond, that has nothing at all to do with the volume of your voice. Repeating yourself louder only teaches your dog he doesn't have to respond to cues the first time you give them.

If your dog is barking and you start yelling to try to get him to stop barking, you will usually only make the barking worse. Your dog probably thinks you are joining in the fun of barking at something exciting, or that you are trying to help him chase away something scary. Even if you are giving him a cue to stop barking, if you yell so you can "be heard" over his barks, the terse, excited tone of your voice may trump the actual words you say, keeping him aroused instead of calming him down. When your dog is barking, it is far more effective to calmly and quietly give him his cue to stop barking than it is to yell at him to be quiet.

Take advantage of your dog's natural radar for quiet, prey-like sounds. Don't raise your voice above a normal conversational volume when you try to interrupt his barking. Make a pssst sound (as in, "Pssst—Hey! Buddy! You wanna buy a solid gold Rolex watch? I got a few here in my trench coat for ten bucks each!"), smack your lips together in an exaggerated kissing sound, or make some other unusual, quiet noise to try to catch your dog's attention when he is barking. The key here is to be calm and quiet. Dogs feed off our emotions, so the calmer you remain, the better your chances will be of calming your dog down. If your dog is overly aroused, he may not be able to respond to your cue. But by staying calm and quiet, at least you are not making the situation worse. As you are quietly talking to him, gently start moving him farther away from whatever he is barking at to help him stop barking. Distance is *always* your friend when you need to calm your dog down. At some point, you will be far enough away that your dog will be able and willing to stop barking and reengage with you.

### Close the drapes

If your herding dog is one who likes to look out the window and bark at everything that moves past your property, you may need to engage in some creative interior design to manage his behavior while you are simultaneously teaching him to be quiet on cue. If your dog can't see or hear what is passing by your house, he can't possibly bark at it. Because you can only control his behavior directly when you are actually with him, you need to find ways to manage his environment so he can't scan the world outside and bark when you aren't around.

The easiest way to keep your dog from barking at things passing by your window is simply to keep him away from the window when you aren't in the room with him. Close the doors to rooms with windows that face sidewalks and busy streets, close the drapes in those rooms, or use gating if you have an open floor plan, to keep your dog physically away from the windows. Crate him with a tasty bone for short periods of time or put him in another room when you are gone so he can't sneak a peek out the windows and bark uncontrollably when you are not there. Consider rearranging furniture temporarily to make access to the windows more difficult or less comfortable for him. Anything you can do to control his access to the windows will support the actual training you do to get his barking under control. Accept that you may never completely eliminate the occasional barking fit when you aren't with your dog, particularly if your dog has free access to watch the world go by when he is alone. Even a well-trained dog will still bark occasionally. But through consistent management, you can certainly minimize his barking when you aren't around, and management and training together will help your dog learn to better control his urge to bark when he is with you.

*If your dog can comfortably lounge on the back of the sofa and watch the world go by, he will probably see plenty of things to bark at when you aren't around.*

## Keep quiet and keep movin'

This technique is very similar to Keep Calm and Move On in Chapter 7. If you are out walking your dog and he starts barking at something, the most immediately useful thing you can do is keep quiet and keep your dog movin'! Too often, as soon as a dog's mouth opens, his owner's feet stop moving and his mouth opens, too. The owner freezes in place and starts to yell over the top of his dog, trying to get him to be quiet. But by stopping and yelling as soon as your dog starts barking, you are teaching him several lessons that will make teaching him to be quiet even more difficult. If your dog is barking because he is scared, your yelling may make him think you are scared, too, further reinforcing his fear and quite possibly increasing the intensity of his barking in the future, when he is in similar situations. If your dog is barking because he is excited or wants to control whatever he's barking at, you are teaching him that barking will get you to stop so he can continue looking and barking at exciting things. Your yelling is telling him that you are really excited, too. You are actually rewarding the very behavior you are trying to change. And when you stop near a distraction, you are tempting your dog to try to physically control it if his herding instincts really start to kick in. Who is actually in charge in this situation? Don't forget that every time you interact with your dog, at least one of you is learning something. Be sure your herding dog isn't training you when you are together. If your dog starts barking, take charge of the situation and quietly keep moving to get distance between your dog and whatever he is barking at, as quickly as possible.

# Training exercises

Teaching your dog to stop barking on cue is mandatory for any dog owner living in an urban setting. If your dog mindlessly barks, he is a nuisance not only to you, but also to everyone within earshot. Helping your herding dog control his vocalizations will help you maintain cordial relations with your neighbors while keeping your home atmosphere more relaxed for everyone to live in. Don't forget, your dog can be a barking nuisance to others when you aren't at home; use management techniques to address that problem.

## Speak with quiet

**Exercise Goal:** Your herding dog will learn to bark and to stop barking on cue.

Teaching your dog to bark on cue is the first step in teaching him to be quiet on cue. Dogs learn well by contrast; pairing "Speak" with "Quiet" will help you teach your dog both cues quickly and effectively.

1.  This is one exercise that you will want to train in a distracting area where you know your dog will see something that he will bark at. This could be at the park or in your living room near a window; anywhere he has thrown a barking fit in the past is a potential training location for this exercise. Put him on leash, even if you are training in your house, and

have some extremely tempting treats ready to use. These treats need to be more valuable to your dog than whatever he might bark at, so you may need to use tidbits of cheese or real meat for this training. The stickier the treat, the longer it will take him to consume and the longer his barking will be physically interrupted. If your dog really likes peanut butter or squeeze cheese, a blob of either stuck on a spoon so he can lick it off is the best type of treat for this exercise. If your dog is too aroused to eat when he starts barking, substitute a toy that he will interact with. If he is holding a toy in his mouth, he can't simultaneously bark. Select rewards for this exercise that will physically help him interrupt his barking.

*A gooey mix of peanut butter and dog treats on a large kitchen spoon makes a perfect sticky reward for being quiet.*

2.  Quietly walk with your dog through the park or sit with him near the living room window and wait for something to trigger him to bark. This is one time you actually want to burst his bubbles you have been protecting since Chapter 7, and allow him to bark, so you can use that opportunity to put his barking behavior on cue. You may need to experiment with training in different locations until you can find one with enough excitement to trigger barking. If your dog barks when your doorbell rings, you

can use that sound for this exercise as well. You might only be able to do one or two repetitions per training session before your dog starts to get so excited that it is difficult to disrupt his barking, or he settles down and quits barking on his own. Don't worry! One or two successful repetitions per training session will help you achieve your training goals faster than no repetitions will.

3. For this exercise, you will use your verbal cue right from the beginning. Barking isn't a behavior with a lot of discrete steps; either your dog barks or he doesn't. By the time you hear your dog bark, the individual bark is already finished. There are no slow or halfway-finished barks or silences to worry about associating with your verbal cues, like there are slow, incomplete, or otherwise less-than-ideal behaviors in the early stages of teaching your dog to lie down or walk politely on leash. Your dog is either barking or not barking. You won't weaken your verbal cues by unintentionally associating them with less-than-perfect performance if you use them right from the start of this exercise, before your dog really understands what you want. Just delay using the cue until the dog starts barking or quits barking. As soon as your dog starts barking, quietly and calmly tell him "Speak." Allow him to bark just two or three times. You need to keep these sessions very, very short. You don't want your dog to get so excited while he's barking that he quits listening to you. Initially, you will be saying your cue just after he starts barking; but with enough repetitions, he will connect your cue with his barking and will start to bark when you tell him to "Speak," even if there is nothing exciting around. After two or three barks, start backing away from the distraction, praising and feeding him his extra-special, extra-sticky treats while you create distance between you and the distraction that triggered the barking. As soon as he stops barking to take his treat, quietly and calmly tell him "Quiet," then continue to praise and feed him several licks of the spoon in a row to keep him quiet. Again, you will start out giving him the cue immediately after he quits barking, but he will soon figure out that "Quiet" means something really good is going to come from you, so it is worth his while to quit barking and start moving toward you. If he starts barking again as you are backing away from the distraction, quietly continue increasing the distance until he settles back down. The first few times you work on this, you may have to move quite a distance away from the distraction to get your dog to be quiet after he starts barking, so be prepared to keep going until he quits barking. Try not to be quite so close to whatever he is barking at the next repetition, so he can settle down more quickly. Be sure to say "Quiet" the moment he stops barking and immediately offer him a treat or toy to prevent him from starting to bark again. If you are ringing the doorbell to trigger his barking, don't have anyone open the

door. Act as if you didn't even hear the bell ring, and disrupt his barking after a few barks by praising and feeding him his treats.

4. You can also use unplanned barking moments to train "Speak" and "Quiet" at home. If your dog is looking out the window and starts barking unexpectedly, go into the room he is in, cue him to "Speak," allow two or three more barks, then pick him up (if he is small) or gently lead him by the collar away from the window. As soon as he quits barking, tell him "Quiet" and praise him profusely as you work your way toward your stash of dog treats or his favorite toy. As long as you continue to praise your dog as you immediately move toward the other reward, he will understand that both rewards are linked to him being quiet.

5. As your dog becomes more fluent with "Speak" and "Quiet," you will be able to disrupt his behavior by calmly telling him "Quiet," without needing to move farther away from the distraction that triggered the barking. Have patience; this may take a long time to accomplish, but it certainly can be accomplished! Don't be stingy with your rewards for this behavior. It is very difficult for an aroused herding dog to suppress his natural inclination to bark. Remember that rewards aren't just treats. You can give praise, pet him, give him his favorite toy, let him outside or, occasionally, actually tell him "Speak," allowing him to bark a few more times at the distraction as his reward for a good "Quiet" behavior. Your dog should never know for sure what he is going to get as a reward for being quiet, but he should be able to count on the fact that you will give him some type of meaningful reward every time he listens to you and stops barking on cue. He might even start to self-disrupt his barking after a few barks in anticipation of a reward. Don't forget to reward that silence even though you didn't ask for it! At the very least, be sure to praise your dog and let him know you sincerely appreciate his display of self-control if he stops barking without your cue.

You can use "Speak" as a reward for other behaviors once you've taught "Quiet." It takes energy to bark and is self-soothing to your dog, so it is a great reward to allow him to bark a little after performing a difficult or stressful behavior. Barking helps elevate a dog's attitude as well and can get him in the mood to work together with you. "Speak" is also one of those timeless dog tricks that is fun to teach and show off.

## Park it redux

**Exercise Goal:** Your herding dog goes to his mat and quietly stays there when the doorbell rings.

Teaching your dog to remain calm and quiet when people come into your home is an effort your houseguests will thank you for undertaking. One handy application of the Park It exercise in Chapter 8 is to provide your dog a job to do instead of barking and jumping on people as they come into your home. For this exercise, your dog is going to learn an additional cue that tells him to go to his mat and stay there quietly until he is released. He will learn that the sound of the doorbell or a knock on the door (or both, if you prefer) is a cue to go to his mat and quietly wait there to be released.

We are teaching Lassie to be polite when family and friends come over. Please be patient! It may take us a little longer to answer the door while we work on this! Thanks!

*If you are concerned guests will become impatient while you work through this exercise, make a fun sign to put on your front door while you are teaching your dog how to greet guests politely. This will let people know that it may take you a little longer to come to the door while you are training.*

1.  Thoroughly work through the Park It exercise in Chapter 8 before starting this exercise. Your dog should already understand how to go to his mat from across the room and to stay on it until he is released. If your dog barks uncontrollably at the sound of the doorbell, also work on the Speak with Quiet training before starting this exercise. Decide where you are going to put the mat you want your dog to use when people come into your home. Ideally, this spot is across the room from the door, facing it. That will provide distance between your dog and your guests when they first come into your home, which will make it easier for your dog to stay on his mat, but will still allow him to see what is going on and also allow you to keep an eye on him while you open the door.

2.  Start this exercise with your dog on leash and some tasty treats. Even though your dog should already know how to go across the room to get on his mat without you tossing treats in front of him, you are now using those treats to help him understand that the sound of the doorbell means he should go to his mat. Remember, if he has a long history of barking and going wild when the doorbell rings, it will take some time for him to learn to behave more appropriately.

3.  If you don't have someone who can help you with this exercise, skip down to Step 5. If you do have a helper, you can start with your mat in the final location where you want your dog to go when the doorbell rings. Stand with your dog a few feet from his mat and have your helper stand outside, door closed, and ring the doorbell. As soon as the doorbell rings, give your verbal "Park it" cue and toss a treat on your dog's mat. Your dog should automatically move to get his treat on his mat because of the training you have already done with that behavior. Let him remain on his mat for a few seconds before giving him his release cue. If he starts barking, cue him to be quiet and reward him for doing so before releasing him from his mat. Repeat five times per training session. Your helper remains outside for this step. If your helper can see or hear you without opening the door, have her wait a few seconds after you release your dog and he is completely off his mat before ringing the doorbell again. If your helper can't see or hear what is going on, prearrange to have her ring the doorbell once every thirty to sixty seconds, to give you time to get your dog on and off his mat before it rings again. If something happens and you don't get to complete a repetition before the doorbell rings again, start over wherever you are when the doorbell rings. If your dog is still on his mat, have him continue to stay on it. If he is off the mat for any reason, cue him to go to it again, helping him go to it if necessary.

4.  When your dog is 80% successful going to his mat from a few feet away and staying on it quietly when he hears the doorbell ring and you give your "Park it" cue and toss a treat, gradually increase the distance your dog has to travel to get to his mat without you following right behind him, just like you did when you originally taught this behavior in Step 7 of the Park It exercise. The only difference is you will wait to send your dog to his mat until the doorbell rings. For this step, your helper will remain outside between doorbell rings. Remember to continue to cue and reward quiet behavior on the mat. If your dog goes to his mat but continues to bark uncontrollably after the doorbell rings, don't go to the next step of this exercise until you teach him to remain on the mat quietly. Your dog can't leave the mat until he quits barking. If he fails to respond to your "Quiet" cue, work on "Speak" and "Quiet" without the mat until your dog will stop barking on cue after the doorbell rings.

5.  If you don't have a helper, you have two choices: (1) you can record your own doorbell and use that for your initial training, or (2) you can ring your doorbell yourself. If you use a recording, put your playback device in a handy location so you can quickly turn it on and off. If you ring the doorbell yourself, start with the mat close to the door. Ring the doorbell, then step inside, give your "Park it" cue, and toss a cookie on your dog's mat. This is not as precise as having someone else ring the doorbell for

you, but it will work. Only open the door wide enough to get your hand outside and ring the doorbell, so you can quickly get back inside to toss a treat. Your dog remains inside the house while you do this. Proceed through Steps 3 and 4 of this exercise, slowly moving the mat away from the door toward its final location. It will take a little more physical coordination to train this behavior on your own, but you can definitely accomplish it with a little patience and creativity.

6. Once your dog is reliably going straight to his mat when the doorbell rings, it is time to get rid of the verbal "Park it" cue. Because you have always followed the sound of the doorbell with your "Park it" cue, by now your dog should anticipate hearing that cue when the doorbell rings and start to go to his mat even before you have the chance to say it. For this step, ring the doorbell but delay giving your "Park it" cue; if your dog starts to go to his mat without it, remain quiet. Reward and praise him when he gets to his mat. If he doesn't move toward his mat without your verbal "Park it" cue, continue to pair the doorbell and the cue for a few more training sessions. Wait two seconds after the doorbell rings before giving him the verbal cue until you notice that he is starting to reliably (80% or better) move toward his mat before you give the verbal cue. When he reaches that point, try again to completely eliminate the verbal cue.

7. Now you are ready to add in the door being opened after the doorbell rings. If you have a helper, she will be playing the role of a delivery person who comes to your door and rings the doorbell, but doesn't come inside. Stand near the door with your dog. Have your helper ring the doorbell, or, if you are training alone, reach outside and ring your doorbell or play your doorbell recording. By now, your dog should be going to his mat without you following him when he hears the doorbell ring. When your dog is on his mat, calmly open the door. Stand still near the open door a few seconds, then close the door, walk over to your dog, reward him while he is on his mat, and give him his release cue. If your dog starts barking or leaves his mat before being released, close the door and help him get back on his mat before opening the door again. If your dog doesn't go all the way to his mat when the doorbell rings, help him get on to his mat before going to the door to open it. If he starts barking when the doorbell rings and won't stop on cue, do not open the door. When he stops barking, praise him for a good "Quiet," open the door, and immediately walk over to him and reward him if he remains quiet or stops barking when you give him the quiet cue. If he won't stop barking, close the door and wait for him to stop barking. When he quiets down, open the door, but this time only open it part way, and reward your dog before he has the chance to start barking again.

8. When your dog can remain quietly on his mat while you open the door, it is finally time to let someone come in. If you don't have a helper for this step, skip ahead to Step 11. Start this step by standing close to your dog's mat instead of the door; it may be more difficult for your dog to stay on his mat when someone actually comes in, so you want to be nearby to help him be successful. Have your helper ring the doorbell, wait ten seconds (or however long it usually takes your dog to get on the mat), then open the door herself and come inside. Your helper is now playing the role of a guest. She should not look at or talk to the dog or attempt to pet him; the goal is to get your dog to go to his mat and stay there when a person comes in the house and ignores him. Using the 80% rule, gradually increase the distance between you and your dog's mat. Eventually, you should be able to stand near the door as your guest comes in while your dog goes, by himself, to his mat and waits there quietly for his release cue. If at any time he doesn't go all the way to his mat, he leaves the mat when your helper comes in, or he starts barking and doesn't stop barking on cue, have your helper immediately go back outside and close the door while you help your dog get back on his mat and remain quietly there until he is released. Review the Park It exercise in Chapter 8 if you need help addressing problems with the mat behavior.

9. When your dog is able to stay on his mat quietly while you stand near the door and your helper opens the door herself and comes in, you can start opening the door to let your helper in, as you will in real-life situations. It is a good habit to wait until your dog is on his mat before you open the door to increase the likelihood he won't get distracted by the door opening, and stop short of his mat. Remember to keep an eye on your dog while you open the door, though. If he leaves his mat at any point before you give him your release cue, have your helper leave (if she is already inside), and close the door while you help your dog get back on his mat. The only way your dog should get attention from anyone coming into your home is by staying on his mat until he is released.

10. The last step in this exercise is to have your helper approach your dog while he quietly stays on his mat. The attention he gets from your helper becomes the reward your dog gets for going to his mat and staying there without barking. Remember the mat rules, though. Your dog can move around while he is being approached, but he can't leave the mat until you give him his release cue. Your helper should stand close enough that she can interact with your dog without your dog leaving the mat. Keep the initial interaction low-key. Your helper should not give much direct eye contact or encourage excited activity. Once your dog has been greeted, your helper should quietly walk away. Be prepared to help your dog stay quiet and on his mat when the helper moves away. This can be difficult

to do if your dog really enjoyed the attention he was getting. If your dog starts barking or jumping on your helper (even if he doesn't leave his mat to do it), have her immediately walk away. Neither of those behaviors should be rewarded with attention; only calm, quiet behavior should result in being greeted by whomever comes through the door. Use the 80% rule to slowly increase the level of excitement your helper shows while greeting your dog. The more exciting she is, the more difficult it will be for your dog to stay on his mat when she leaves. If your dog tries to jump on your helper after being released from his mat, put a leash on him before repeating the exercise. To prevent him from jumping, pick the leash up before releasing him and calmly cue him to be quiet. If he remains calm and quiet, your helper can return and pet him some more; if he gets excited or starts to jump, your helper should ignore him and leave.

11. If you don't have a helper you will need to try to play the role of the guest as best you can. After ringing the bell and following your dog to his mat, spend some time petting and praising him in an excited manner, similar to how most guests greet your dog. You are substituting your excitement for the extra excitement of a guest, so try to make the training as realistic as possible. If he starts barking or tries to leave his mat, calmly and quietly put him back on it before petting him again. Then walk away a few steps before giving him his release cue. If he tries to leave the mat to follow you or becomes too excited after you release him, quietly put him back on the mat, and take fewer steps away before releasing him to help him remain calmer when he is released. This isn't as efficient as having another person to help you with this step, but your dog will eventually learn to stay on his mat when he is approached. Just be sure to take advantage of any training opportunities you have when guests do come over to help him learn to stay on his mat and remain calm.

12. When your dog will quietly stay on his mat while either your helper pets him and then walks away or, if you don't have a helper, you excitedly interact with him on his mat and then walk away, you can start to use this new door behavior when actual guests come to your home. While your dog is learning that these rules apply to anyone coming into your home, be sure to put a leash on him before you open the door so it will be easier to help him get on his mat. If you don't believe your dog will stay on his mat across the room while you open the door, your dog isn't ready to start this step in the training. If you think your dog is ready, but nevertheless don't want to take the extra time to help your dog get on his mat before opening the door to guests, move his mat closer to the door so you can accomplish both in a timely manner. If you do not enforce the mat behavior every time the doorbell rings, your dog may eventually learn he doesn't really have to go to his mat every time he hears the doorbell, and

all your hard work up to this point will start to come undone. If you don't have the mat in place or have the time to work the behavior before opening the door, at least put your dog in another room or outside before you open the door so he can't continue to practice the unacceptable door behaviors you are trying to change. This will still weaken the doorbell cue somewhat, because your dog will hear the sound but not be expected to go to his mat, but that is better than not expecting him to go to his mat *and* allowing him to bark or jump on guests as he did in the past. Life does not always provide perfect training scenarios. Make the best of imperfect training situations and then get back on track with your training plan as soon as possible. Be sure to ask guests to approach your dog calmly and quietly, or to ignore him altogether. Guests should give rather matter-of-fact, brief greetings to help your dog maintain his self-control and stay on his mat. Instruct guests to immediately walk away and ignore the dog if he jumps up or gets off his mat. Even if a guest says, "It's okay! I don't mind if your dog jumps up on me!" insist that your dog must remain on his mat. Your dog won't understand what your guest is saying. He will only understand that he is still allowed to jump on some people, so he will continue to try to jump on every person who comes over to pet him.

Barking is as natural to dogs as talking is natural to people. Dogs communicate all kinds of information to us if we really listen to the barks. Barking is a controllable behavior, but not an extinguishable one. Be considerate to your neighbors by taking the time to teach your dog to control his barking and to your guests by teaching your dog to be calm and quiet when they come to your home. Most of all, be kind to your dog by giving him opportunities to express himself as a dog from time to time, and life will be more pleasant for everyone!

# Chapter 10

# Management and Training for Exceptional Energy and Über-Intelligence

*Well may the shepherd feel an interest in his dog: he it is indeed that earns the family bread, of which he is himself, with the smallest morsel, always grateful and always ready to exert his utmost abilities in his master's interests.*

*James Hogg, aka the Ettrick Shepherd*
*Scottish poet and novelist*

Herding dogs are known for amazing feats of intelligence and incredible displays of physical prowess. There is absolutely no question that when you own a herding dog, you own an extremely intelligent, energetic, problem-solving canine workmate. But with the privilege of owning this type of dog comes great responsibility; if that body isn't exercised and that brain in your herding dog's head isn't put to good use on a regular basis, you might just end up with the type of dog who stars in the horror stories that pop up regularly about under-exercised, under-stimulated herding dogs who thoroughly destroy walls, floors, furniture, fences, themselves, and anything else they decide to focus on in a futile attempt to relieve their boredom. Exercise and training are crucial to successfully living with a herding dog, particularly when your dog has no traditional herding work to do.

## Management techniques

### Keeping weight off

The role physical exercise plays in modifying a herding dog's behavior has been discussed in earlier chapters. A fit and well-exercised dog is healthier and better able to focus on learning than a dog who is ready to explode because he's been cooped up in the house all day and has tons of pent-up energy to burn. But the benefit of exercise will be lost if your herding dog is overweight.

Being overweight puts unnecessary stress on hips and elbows, which is particularly concerning for breeds prone to hip dysplasia. Keeping your herding dog at a healthy weight will not guarantee he will never become arthritic or dysplastic, but it will make it easier for him to remain mobile if he does. Many dogs will naturally put on extra weight as they grow older and their metabolisms begin to slow; exercise and dietary management become even more important as your herding dog ages. Be sure to consult with your veterinarian for advice on proper weight and nutrition for your older dog. A healthy herding dog is muscular and can move with ease; typically you see at least a slight tuck (the dog equivalent of a waist) and can readily feel his ribs without putting much pressure on his rib cage, even on squarer-built breeds like Australian Cattle Dogs and Pembroke Welsh Corgis. If your dog has no waist at all, can't sustain a trot for very long without becoming winded, or has difficulty standing up and lying down, consult with your veterinarian to develop a plan to get him to a healthier weight and to check for any other health issues. There are many reliable online veterinary resources to help you understand how to talk with your veterinarian about your dog's weight. Being fat is not a sign of a loved dog; it is a sign of a dog whose life is potentially being prematurely shortened by the extra pounds he is forced to carry around.

*Even if your dog is a stout herding breed, like an Australian Cattle Dog, or one with a considerable coat, like an Old English Sheepdog, you should be able to see or feel some muscle definition, his ribs should be relatively easy to feel, and a tuck should be apparent when looking at your dog both from the side and from the top.*

## Traditional and not-so-traditional herding dog exercise activities

Providing adequate physical exercise for a herding dog can prove to be a challenge for a busy dog owner, but it is absolutely necessary for his mental and physical well-being. If no one in your family can exercise your dog, it may be necessary to hire someone else to exercise him. If you cannot or will not make the commitment to exercising your herding dog every day, reconsider getting a dog who needs a lot of exercise to be healthy and happy. Other pets might be more appropriate if you have a sedentary or chaotic lifestyle. A tank of beautiful fish or a small songbird might be a better pet choice for you than a herding dog who demands daily vigorous exercise.

When a herding dog doesn't get enough exercise, he may resort to barking, digging, jumping, chewing, and nipping to help him burn off his excess energy. These are all issues that can make training more challenging than necessary. While you may think that taking a brisk walk around the block twice a day or letting your dog out into the backyard to run around by himself is adequate exercise, it doesn't provide anything close to the same amount of exercise that running him for several miles or letting him swim or retrieve tennis balls does. Being alone in your yard will rarely motivate your dog to exercise himself, unless he comes across something he believes needs to be herded. Even having two or more dogs doesn't eliminate the need to provide organized exercise, since most adult herding dogs only play together in short spurts. Daily vigorous exercise is just as important as food, water, shelter, veterinary care, training, and love to the overall health of your dog. With regular exercise, most people notice a decrease in many of their dogs' behavioral problems. A tired herding dog is far from a perfect herding dog, but he is certainly a happier dog who will be much easier to live with and train.

A healthy herding dog at proper weight can easily run *at least* one mile twice a day and still have plenty of energy left over to train, play, and keep up with the family. The longer-legged, bigger herding dogs can easily handle two or three miles. *Continuous physical exertion* is the important concept here. Walking a few miles or even allowing the dog to do stop-and-start running off leash does not produce the same physical effects that running at a consistent speed for a significant period of time will produce. Walking is certainly better than no exercise at all, but consider other options to give your herding dog more appropriate exercise, if possible. Jogging is a far more effective exercise option than walking. Biking is also a great option for many people; using a bike attachment such as a Springer® will allow you to safely bike with your dog without holding on to his leash. If at all possible, run or bike in an area where you can keep your dog on grass, dirt, or other soft surfaces, to minimize stress on his joints. Stair walking, both up and down, is good exercise, particularly if you have access to long flights of stairs, such as those found in a sports stadium. Walking in sand, water, snow, or through heavy vegetation will help increase the effort your dog needs to exert as he moves. Walking against more resistance will provide him more exercise than merely walking down the sidewalk at a leisurely pace. Canicross, scootering, skijoring, horseback riding, hiking, and even canine treadmill work are also great exercise options, with proper training.

*Even the short-legged herding breeds, like the Cardigan Welsh Corgi, need considerable exercise every day to be healthy and happy. Sully can keep up with the horses and Dalmatians quite well when he goes out for his daily excursions with the gang.*

In warmer weather, swimming or running through water will quickly wear your dog out. Swimming and retrieving in shallow water are both excellent forms of exercise that do not put much stress on joints. Always start slowly and carefully with any water activity until your dog knows how to swim. Walk with your dog on leash in shallow water, gradually increasing the depth until he just loses contact with the bottom. Allow him to figure out on his own how to move his body and swim at this depth before allowing him off leash or in deeper water. Always stand closer to the shore than your dog so you are in the shallower water and can safely help him if he gets in trouble while he is learning how to swim. If in doubt, put a dog life jacket on him. A panicked dog poses a very real drowning threat to a human swimmer so be cautious about water rescues. Life jackets and long lines are the safest ways to help your dog get comfortable in the water and help him if he gets in trouble. If your dog doesn't actually swim, tossing floating toys into shallow water for him to retrieve will increase the amount of exercise your dog gets, because running through the shallow water will be more difficult than running on dry land. Just make sure there aren't sharp rocks, broken glass, or other hazards in the water that could hurt your dog. Also, be sure to keep current on any news of potentially toxic algal or bacterial blooms in your area and keep your dog out of any water that might be contaminated. Even if he doesn't swallow water when he is swimming, he could still possibly ingest contaminated water off his fur. Use your common sense when picking a swimming hole for your herding dog. If you would not, or should not, swim in the water, don't allow your dog to swim in it, either.

*Running and playing in water gives Shishka plenty of exercise without putting excessive strain on her joints.*

In cold weather, a brief romp through snowdrifts will do the trick to get some additional exercise out of your time outside together. Playing fast games of retrieve, especially if your dog has to run uphill to fetch his toy, is good as long as you keep your dog moving. A horse lunge whip with a fuzzy toy or tennis ball tied to the end makes a great chase toy. Just be sure that you run your dog in large circles in both directions when you play and allow him to occasionally catch and play with the toy he has been chasing. If he never gets the chance to catch the toy, he may simply give up chasing it.

There are also a number of competitive dog sports you can participate in that will help you keep your dog exercised and healthy. Agility, tracking, herding trials, disc dog, canine freestyle, dock diving, competitive obedience, competitive canicross, and treibball are just a few of the dog sports that require routine, physically demanding training to compete in safely and successfully. Even if you never actually compete, engaging in one or more of these sports will help you develop a good working relationship with your dog, allow you to meet other dog owners who share a similar interest in the sport, and keep both you and your dog moving!

*Running with your herding dog in canicross events or organized
road races is a great way for both of you to get exercise!*

Be sure to consult your veterinarian before starting any exercise plan, then start slowly, and gradually build up the amount of exercise you give your dog each day. And don't forget to check with your own doctor before taking up vigorous exercise with your dog, to be sure you are up to the challenge as well. Both you and your dog will benefit from making a commitment to daily exercise.

*Because Bearded Collie Rorie has always been kept at a healthy weight and given adequate daily exercise, she is still able to help her owner move sheep at fifteen years young!*

## Tricks do the trick

One very easy and fun way to give your dog work to do is simply to teach him tricks. This is a "management" technique because most tricks don't teach your dog how to behave in everyday situations. But tricks do require training and can keep your dog mentally active and engaged with you long after you've taught him all the behaviors he needs to know to be an enjoyable canine family member. The list of tricks you can teach your dog is practically endless and many tricks will provide him a considerable degree of physical exercise. Your dog doesn't know the difference between a behavior you teach him simply for your own amusement and a behavior you teach him out of necessity; it's all work to him! You can teach him simple tricks like rolling over, sitting up, or balancing a treat on his nose, or more complex tricks like identifying toys by name, riding a skateboard, or finding hidden items. You can also teach your herding dog to help with simple tasks around the house, like turning lights on and off, carrying lightweight items, or finding car keys. Teaching tricks is a great way to improve your skills as a trainer and strengthen the relationship between you and your dog. Trick training will help you manage all the intelligence and physical energy your herding dog has without the stress sometimes associated with teaching him traditional "obedience" behaviors.

*Imagination, physical ability, and safety are the only limits to the tricks you can teach your dog. Gabriel loves to ride his skateboard.*

There are many informative books and DVDs available to help you train tricks; several of them are listed in the Resources section at the end of this book. YouTube videos and Internet searches will also provide you with ideas and instruction. Selecting tricks that require physical skill or involve behaviors similar to those needed to herd will give you the most bang for your management buck, but training any trick is better than not training at all. To get you started with tricks, try teaching your dog to identify objects by name. As long as you don't run out of unique names for objects, you can teach your dog to pick out many different objects by name.

1. Start this trick with your dog on leash, in a room with no objects on the floor except the ones you are using for training. Cue your dog to sit and calmly put the first object you want to name on the floor a few feet away from your dog. Let your dog see you put a treat on or under the object. Step back beside your dog, give his release cue, and point to the object, encouraging him to go to it to get the treat. Let your dog drag his leash so if he tries to pick up the object and play a game of keep-away, you can easily stop him by picking up his leash. When he reaches the object, say the name you've selected for the object as your dog is getting his treat, and praise him while he eats it. Praise him even more if he picks the

object up and brings it to you. This is not a retrieving game (although you can teach him to retrieve objects by name as another trick), but if he picks up the object, that's okay! As soon as your dog has finished his treat, put another one on or under the object, gently lead your dog a few feet away, and send him to it again. Repeat this five times per training session, and then put the object away until the next training session.

*Help your dog learn to identify objects by keeping him close to the correct object in your initial training sessions.*

2. When your dog goes directly to the object at least 80% of the time after you give him his release cue, begin to say the object's name immediately after you release him from his sit, before he actually gets to the object. Also, eliminate the treat on or under the object and start giving him his reward *after* he goes to the object. Repeat this step five times per training session until your dog will quickly run over to the object when you cue him to "Go find your _____ [ball, bone, rope, or whatever you've named the object]" at least 80% of the time after being released from his sit. Don't let him cheat on his sit while you are training this trick! If he breaks his sit before you give him his release cue, quietly put him back in his original spot and have him sit before releasing him to go to the object again. Always be sure to keep basic obedience skills strong while you teach tricks!

3.  When your dog is going 80% of the time or more to the first object, repeat Steps 1 and 2 with a different object. Be sure to give the second object a different name from the first one. Work with this second object alone until your dog is going to it as he did with the first one. It may be easier for your dog to work through this step if the second object is visually distinct from the first one. For example, if you used a ball for the first object, you could use a rope toy for the second object.

4.  When your dog is 80% reliable going to this second object, you are ready to teach him to discriminate between the two. To start, you will send him to the same object each time during a single training session. For example, if you are using a ball and a rope toy as the two objects, for this step you will send your dog only to the ball, or only to the rope toy, during a single training session. Cue your dog to sit, and then set both objects down, several feet apart and a few feet in front of your dog. Step back beside your dog, pick up his leash, give him his release cue, and tell him to go to find the ball. Point to the ball as you say its name. If he hesitates, quietly wait for him to move toward it, then praise him when he reaches it. If he doesn't make a move toward either object after about ten seconds, gently lead him to a spot a little closer to the ball and give him his cue again while pointing to the ball. If he still doesn't move toward it, or if he tries to go to the wrong object, encourage him to the correct one by pointing to it and acting very interested in it yourself. Be sure to praise when he goes to the correct object, and let him play with it briefly as his reward (or give him a treat, if that is the reward he prefers), as soon as he gets to the object.

5.  Take your dog back to his starting position and cue him to sit. Put the ball in a different position relative to the rope toy, release your dog, and send him to find the ball again. Every time he identifies the ball, put it back in a different position before sending him to find it again. Complete five repetitions with the ball per training session, each repetition in a different place, and then put both objects away so he can't get them when you aren't around. By varying the location of the ball every repetition, you are teaching your dog to identify the ball by sight, not by location (i.e., if the ball is always positioned to the left of the rope toy, your dog may think anything to the left of the rope toy is a "ball" instead of identifying the ball by its appearance regardless of where it is relative to the rope toy).

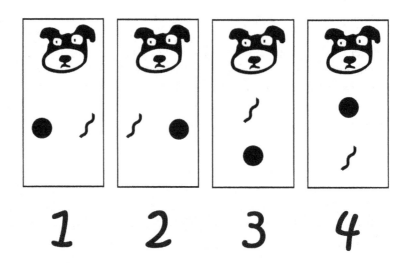

*Vary where you place the objects each time you send your dog to find one of them. This will test whether the dog learned to identify it by its physical characteristics, not its relative location.*

6.  In the next training session, repeat Steps 4 and 5, but this time, only send your dog to the rope toy. Your dog may try to go to the ball because that is the object you sent him to last training session. That's okay; just be prepared to help him select the correct object as you did before.

7.  Continue to send your dog to only one object per training session until your dog is 80% reliable going to the correct object. Pay particular attention to the first repetition you do each training session. If your dog consistently goes to the wrong object on his first try, he is probably remembering the object you sent him to the last training session, rather than listening to which one you are sending him to this training session. Work a little longer on Steps 5 and 6 until your dog is going to the correct object on the first repetition at least 80% of the time. At this point, you can start mixing up which object you send him to, so he has to identify both objects in the same training session. For example, you might send him once to the ball, two times to the rope toy, once again to the ball, and then back to the rope toy in a single training session. Always be prepared to help him make the correct choice. If he is really struggling, move the objects farther apart and go back to focusing on only one object in a training session. As he gets more fluent with distinguishing between the two objects by name, you can gradually move them closer together to make visual discrimination more difficult for him.

8.  When he is 80% correct with selecting either of the objects when you point to the correct one while giving the verbal cue for it, eliminate the arm cue. Stand still and simply cue him to "Go find your _____." He

may still be relying on your hand motion to identify the correct object, so expect some confusion. Resist repeating the cue or pointing to the correct object; instead, if your dog doesn't move toward the correct object within ten seconds, gently move him closer to the correct object, so it will be difficult for him not to see it. Don't forget to put him in a sit and release him before you cue him to go find a particular object. If he breaks his sit before being released, always take him back to his original spot and have him sit again before releasing him to go the object. When your dog can reliably discriminate between the two objects on your verbal cue alone (and probably your eye motion, if you always look at the correct object when you send your dog), you are ready to move on to the next step.

9. Repeat Steps 1 and 2 with a third object. Teach your dog that object's name thoroughly before moving to Step 3. When your dog goes to this new object at least 80% of the time when he is released from his sit, you are ready to teach him to discriminate between this new object and the two he already knows. Start by working through Steps 4 through 8, using two of the three objects in a single training session. You will do some training sessions with the ball and the new object, some sessions with the rope toy and the new object, and a few with the ball and the rope toy. When he can identify objects in pairs correctly 80% of the time, set out all three objects at once and work carefully through Steps 4 through 8 again.

10. When your dog can identify three objects correctly 80% of the time, start back at Step 1 with a fourth object. Continue to add objects, one at a time, as your dog masters the previous ones. Be sure each one has a unique name. The more unique the names sound, the easier it will be for your dog to identify each object by verbal cue only. If you start to lose track of the names you use, make a list! It is very important that you use the same cue for the same object every time you train, so do what you need to do to remember what names you use. Don't limit yourself to using your dog's toys for this trick; anything that your dog can safely interact with is a candidate for identification.

11. If you want to be sure your dog knows his objects by their names alone, face away from them when you give him his cue so you don't unintentionally help him pick the correct one by looking at it, subtly leaning toward it, or holding your breath until he gets to the correct one. Stand with your back toward the objects and have your dog sit in front of you, facing you. Give him his release cue, followed by the object cue, and then wait until he leaves to find the object before you quietly turn around to see if he picks the right one. Be ready to help him if he is confused when you first try this; you may have been inadvertently giving him physical

cues to help him identify the correct object when you stood facing the objects. Now he has to rely strictly on your verbal cue to figure out which object is the correct one. If necessary, work through Steps 4 through 8 again, using two or three objects, but stand with your back toward them to help your dog learn to identify objects by verbal cue alone.

12. Another way to make this trick more challenging for your dog is to increase the distance he has to travel to find an object. Once your dog is doing well identifying a few objects up close, you can start slowly increasing the distance between him and the objects. This will make it increasingly difficult for him to find the correct object, and he will have to remain focused on his task for longer periods of time to be successful. Start by moving him back from the objects, just a foot or two at a time. Be sure he is 80% reliable finding the object at his current distance before increasing it any more. Always be ready to help him if he struggles by quietly moving him closer to where the object is and trying again. You can eventually turn this trick into a search game. Start by sliding the object partially under a rug or piece of furniture, or just around a corner, before sending your dog to find it. Be ready to help him if he gets frustrated or gives up searching, by guiding him closer to the object.

This is just one of thousands of tricks you can teach your dog. Have fun! If you start to train a trick but decide you don't want to continue teaching it, don't go back to training it in your next training session. You may find that certain tricks are too physically difficult for your dog to perform, or they aren't that interesting once you actually start training them. What matters most is that you are doing *something* with your dog that requires him to actively think. Herding requires a lot of intelligence, and dogs must be able to problem solve with a high degree of success in order to protect and move livestock. Teaching your dog various tricks that utilize his problem-solving capacity is a great way to head off problems that can arise from herding dog boredom.

## Training exercises

Even if you are consistent in providing your dog considerable amounts of daily exercise and teach him basic manners and tricks, your herding dog may still be lacking adequate mental exercise. Herding dogs are a versatile bunch and are well suited to many competitive dog sport activities. Everything from traditional obedience competition, agility, tracking, and herding to treibball, nose work, disc dog, and canine freestyle are activities that you and your dog can enjoy together. Training for a dog sport, particularly if you can take classes, will help you commit to consistent training with your dog. You will meet other people who enjoy training their dogs and will benefit from the guidance of your instructor to help you move forward in your dog's training plan. The training exercises you do will vary by sport, but they all will provide physical and mental challenges to your dog that will help keep him healthy and having fun working with you. Training clubs, private instructors, and the Internet are all good sources of information about various dog sports and training opportunities for you and your dog. Even if you live in the city, there are many opportunities to participate in actual herding training, if you are willing and able to drive to the country to work with working herding dog trainers.

Several dog sports are particularly popular with herding dog owners. Agility is probably the most popular; Border Collies, Shetland Sheepdogs, and other herding breeds make up a large percentage of dogs competing in this obstacle-course-based activity. Their physical dexterity, ability to problem solve, and willingness to work at a distance from their handlers help these breeds excel in the sport. There are many training clubs and private trainers who provide agility classes. If you want to train your herding dog for competitive agility, you will either need to own, or have regular access to, several different large, specialized, expensive pieces of agility equipment (along with enough space to set them up and use them for training) so you can practice between classes. And both you and your dog must be physically able to negotiate agility courses safely and within the time allowed (sometimes in less than one minute). There are many videos on YouTube that show different types of agility classes and trials if you are interested in learning more.

Another popular dog sport that is a little less equipment-intensive is traditional competitive obedience. In this sport, precision is important. Teams complete a standard set of obedience exercises every time they compete, and are scored according to how close they come to the perfect combination of precision and teamwork, as described in detail in the rules for the sport. Herding dogs make excellent obedience partners because they can be taught quite precise behaviors. A variation of this sport is rally obedience. In this sport, teams move from printed sign to printed sign, performing the behaviors written on each one. Although the performance precision required in rally obedience isn't as strict as it is in traditional obedience, the behaviors required are more varied. There are more signs for each level of rally obedience than are used in a single rally competition course. Every time you compete in rally obedience, you and your dog will perform an entirely new course made up of a subset of the signs, so you never do the same course twice. Rally obedience tends to appeal more to handlers who thrive on competitive variety or who aren't interested in training to the level of precision required in traditional competitive obedience.

There are many other activities besides agility and obedience that herding dogs can excel in with proper training. The Resources section at the end of the book has information on several. To keep your dog happy and healthy, you need to commit to exercising his body and brain regularly. Finding a sport that appeals to both of you will make keeping that commitment fun!

*Herding dogs make fantastic competition partners. But even if you never step inside a competition ring with your dog, training for one or more dog sports is a great way to keep your herding dog busy and expand your circle of friends to include others who love their dogs as much as you love yours!*

# Conclusion

*It is a truism to say that the dog is largely what his master makes of him. He can be savage and dangerous, untrustworthy, cringing and fearful; or he can be faithful and loyal, courageous and the best of companions and allies.*

*Sir Ranulph Fiennes*
*British explorer*

Life with herding dogs is always exciting and, at times, can be quite challenging. The instincts that allowed their ancestors to work and thrive in challenging agrarian environments are often useless in the comfortable urban environs most of us now share with our dogs. These instincts can present training challenges that may, at first, seem too difficult to overcome. By adopting a more herding-dog-centric view of the world, and working *with* your dog's instincts, rather than against them, you can teach your dog how to behave more appropriately in your home without expecting him to become something he can't ever be. He might just teach you a thing or two about the strength and beauty of the canine-human bond along the way. And isn't that bond really why you chose to bring a herding dog into your home in the first place?

# Appendix

## Breeds Used to Assist with Herding Livestock

Airedale Terrier

Altdeutsche Hütehunde (Tiger, Gelbbacke, Harzer Fuchs, Kuh-hund, Schafpudel, Schwarzer, Strobel)

American Eskimo

Appenzeller Sennenhund

Australian Cattle Dog

Australian Kelpie

Australian Shepherd

Australian Stumpy Tail Cattle Dog

Basque Shepherd Dog

Bearded Collie

Beauceron

Belgian Shepherd Dog (Groenendael, Laekenois, Tervuren, Malinois)

Bergamasco Sheepdog

Berger Picard

Berger Blanc Suisse

Berger de Savoie

Bernese Mountain Dog

Blue Heeler

Blue Lacy

Border Collie

Bouvier des Ardennes

Bouvier des Flandres

Briard

Can de Palleiro

Canaan Dog

Cane de Oropa

Cane Paratore

Cão de Fila de Sao Miguel

Cão da Serra de Aires

Cardigan Welsh Corgi

Carea Leonés

Carpathian Shepherd Dog

Catahoula Leopard Dog

Chien Berger de Crau

Chodsky Pes

Croatian Sheepdog

Cumberland Sheepdog

Cur (Blackmouth, Mountain)

Dakotah Shepherd

Danish Farmdog

Dutch Shepherd

English Shepherd

Entlebucher Sennenhund

Farm Collie / Farm Shepherd

Fila Brasileiro

Finnish Lapphund

German Shepherd Dog

Giant Schnauzer

Greater Swiss Mountain Dog

Hairy Mouth Heeler

Hovawart

Huntaway

Icelandic Sheepdog

Keeshond

Kerry Blue Terrier

King Shepherd

Koolie

Lancashire Heeler

Lapponian Herder

McNab

Miniature American Shepherd

Miniature Australian Shepherd

Mudi

Nenets Reindeer Dog

New Zealand Heading Dog

Norwegian Buhund

Old English Sheepdog

Ovejero Magellánico

Ovelheiro Gaúcho

Pastor da Mantiqueira

Patagonian Shepherd

Pembroke Welsh Corgi

Picardy Shepherd

Polski Owczarek Nizinny

Pomeranian Sheepdog

Poodle

Puli

Pumi

Pyrenean Shepherd

Red Heeler

Reindeer Herder

Rottweiler

Rough Collie

Samoyed

Šarplaninac

Savoy Shepherd

Schapendoes

Schipperke

Scotch Collie

Shetland Sheepdog

Shiloh Shepherd

Sinka

Smithfield

Smooth Collie

Soft-Coated Wheaten Terrier

Spanish Water Dog

Standard Schnauzer

Stumpy Tail Cattle Dog

Swedish Lapphund

Swedish Vallhund

Tibetan Terrier

Welsh Sheepdog

Westerwälder Kuhhund

White Swiss Shepherd

# Resources

*Outside of a dog, a book is a man's best friend. Inside of a dog, it is too dark to read.*

*Groucho Marx*

## Recommended reading and cited works

Aloff, Brenda. *Canine Body Language: A Photographic Guide*. Collierville, TN, Fundcraft, Inc., 2005. Comprehensive visual guide to all aspects of canine body language.

American Association of Pet Dog Trainers. *Top Tips from Top Trainers: 1001 Practical Tips and Techniques for Successful Dog Care and Training*. Neptune City, NJ, T.F.H. Publications, Inc., 2010. Information covers a wide range of behavior and training information for pet dog owners.

Antoniak-Mitchell, Dawn. *Terrier-Centric Dog Training: From Tenacious to Tremendous*. Wenatchee, WA, Dogwise Publishing, 2013. Management and training techniques useful for working terriers.

Antoniak-Mitchell, Dawn. *From Birdbrained to Brilliant: Training the Sporting Dog to Be a Great Companion*. Wenatchee, WA, Dogwise Publishing, 2014. Management and training techniques useful for sporting dogs.

Bishop, Sylvia. *It's Magic: Training Your Dog with Sylvia Bishop*. UK, Sylvia Bishop, 1985. Unique, hands-on approach to training all types of dogs for Euro-style competitive obedience.

Bloeme, Peter, and Jeff Perry. *Disc Dogs! The Complete Guide*. Atlanta, GA, Hyperflite, Inc., 2008. Introduction to training and competing in disc dog competitions.

156

Cauis, Johannes. *Of English Dogges—The Diversities, the Names, the Natures, and the Properties*. First edition London, UK, Richard Johnes, 1576, as reprinted, Warwickshire, UK, Vintage Dog Books, 2005. Reprint of one of the earliest-known descriptions of dogs in the English language.

Coppinger, Raymond, and Lorna Coppinger. *Dogs: A New Understanding of Canine Origin, Behavior, and Evolution*. Chicago, IL, University of Chicago Press, 2001. Outstanding presentation of issues relating to the canine-human bond.

Coren, Stanley. "Canine Intelligence—Breed Does Matter" in *Psychology Today*, July 15, 2009 (online). Article explaining canine intelligence assessment.

Coren, Stanley. *The Intelligence of Dogs*. New York, NY, Bantam Books, 1994. Easy-to-read explanation of the various ways to assess canine intelligence.

Cummins, Bryan D. *Colonel Richardson's Airedales: The Making of the British War Dog School 1900–1918*. Calgary, Alberta, CAN, Detselig Enterprises Ltd., 2003. Detailed description of the development of the British military canine program, including the use of various dog breeds.

Dalziel, Hugh. *British Dogs—Their Varieties, History, Characteristics, Breeding, Management and Exhibition*. First edition, London, UK, Alfred Bradley, 1888, as reprinted, London, UK, Ersham Press, 2007. Reprint of a late eighteenth-century book describing contemporary dog breeds.

Darnell, Gerianne. *Canine Crosstraining: Achieving Excellence in Multiple Dog Sports*. Council Bluffs, IA, 2015. Information about simultaneously training for various dog sports.

Daubenton, Louis-Jean-Marie. *Instruction pour les Bergers et les Propriétaires de Troupeaux*. Self-published, 1782. (In French). Topics related to eighteenth-century sheep herding and care presented in a series of questions and answers.

Delta Society. *Professional Standards for Dog Trainers: Effective, Humane Principles*. Renton, WA, Delta Society, 2001. Standard of professional conduct designed to provide a framework for effective, humane dog training.

Donaldson, Jean. *The Culture Clash*. Berkeley, CA, James & Kenneth Publishers, 1996. Easy-to-read exploration of why humans and canines often have communication problems and how to communicate in a more effective way with your dog.

Dunbar, Ian. *Barking*. Berkeley, CA, Center for Applied Animal Behavior, 1986. Easy-to-read primer on barking problems.

Drury, W. D. *British Dogs: Their Points, Selection, and Show Preparation*. New York, NY, Charles Scribner's Sons, 1903. Interesting early-twentieth-century descriptions of various types of breeds popular at that time in the British Isles.

Franklin, Adrian. *Animals and Modern Cultures: A Sociology of Human-Animal Relations in Modernity*. London, UK, Sage Publications, 1999. Overview of present-day relationships with animals.

Ganley, Dee. *Changing People Changing Dogs: Positive Solutions for Difficult Dogs*. Chipping Campden, UK, Learning About Dogs, Ltd., 2006. Information on assessing the causes of canine behavioral problems and clicker-based behavioral modification plans.

Garrett, Susan. *Ruff Love*. Chicopee, MA, Hadley Printing Company, Inc., 2002. Very detailed program to develop a strong working relationship between dog and handler.

Haggerty, Captain. *How to Teach Your Dog to Talk*. New York, NY, Simon & Schuster, 2000. Trick training in an easy-to-follow format.

Hall, Libby. *Postcard Dogs*. London, UK, Bloomsbury Publishing, 2004. Interesting historical collection of late-eighteenth- and early-nineteenth-century dog images, including many herding breeds.

Hancock, David. *Old Farm Dogs*. Risborough, UK, Shire Publications Ltd., 1999. Synopsis of historical farm dog breeds and uses.

Hoffmann, L. *Das Buch vom gesunden und kraken Hund*. Wein, Osterrich, Verlag con Moritz Perles, 1902. (In German). A description of German dog breeds.

Jager, Theodore. *Scout, Red Cross and Army Dogs*. Rochester, NY, Arrow Printing Company, Corp., 1914. Training guide for early-twentieth-century military working dogs.

Jensen, Per, Ed. *The Behavioural Biology of Dogs*. Trowbridge, UK, CABI Publishing, 2008. Collection of articles written by international experts on canine behavior.

Leighton, Robert. *Dogs and All About Them*. London, UK, Cassell and Company Ltd., 1910. Interesting turn-of-the-century historical perspective on various dog breeds, including herding breeds.

Lindsay, Steven. *Handbook of Applied Dog Behavior and Training: Vol. 1 Adaptation and Learning*. Ames, IA, Iowa State Press, 2000. Scholarly work on research and findings related to how canines evolved and how the canine brain works.

Lindsay, Steven. *Handbook of Applied Dog Behavior and Training: Vol. 2 Etiology and Assessment of Behavior Problems*. Ames, IA, Iowa State Press, 2000. Scholarly work on research related to the physical basis and identification of canine behavioral problems.

Lindsay, Steven. *Handbook of Applied Dog Behavior and Training: Vol. 3 Procedures and Protocols*. Ames, IA, Iowa State Press, 2000. Scholarly work on research and findings related to the theory of cynopraxis and behavioral modification.

London, Karen. *Feeling Outnumbered? How to Manage and Enjoy Your Multi-Dog Household*. Black Earth, WI, Dog's Best Friend Ltd., 2001. Useful ideas for successfully living with multiple dogs.

Marschark, Eve. "Nature and Nurture of the Sheep Herding Dog" in *The APDT Chronicle of the Dog*, Vol. 13, No. 3, May/June 2005, pp. 3–7. Succinct explanation of the use of herding behaviors as secondary reinforcers when training herding dogs.

McConnell, Patricia. "Training Outside the Box" in *The Bark*, Nov/Dec 2008, pp. 31–33. Introduction to the role breed instincts play in behavior.

Morris, Desmond. *Dogs: The Ultimate Dictionary of Over 1,000 Dog Breeds*. North Pomfret, VT, Trafalgar Square Publishing, 2001. Well-illustrated and informative general reference book on dog breeds throughout the world.

North, Franklin. "Old Shep and the Central Park Sheep" in *St. Nicholas*, August, 1884. Written for contemporary children, explaining the use of sheep and a Border Collie in Central Park.

Price, Carol. *Collie Psychology: Inside the Border Collie Mind*. Chepstow, UK, First Stone Publishing, 2013. Unique and insightful information on the Border Collie.

Pryor, Karen. *Don't Shoot the Dog: The New Art of Teaching and Training*. Revised edition, New York, NY, Bantam Books, 1999. Revised edition of the classic work on operant conditioning and clicker training.

Pugnetti, Gino. *Cani*. Milan, IT, Mondadori Electa S.p.A., 2003. (In Italian). Interesting contemporary reference book of European dog breeds, including herding breeds.

Ray, Mary, and Justine Harding. *Dog Tricks: Fun and Games for Your Clever Canine*. San Diego, CA, Octopus Publishing Group Ltd., 2005. Basic and advanced tricks with step-by-step photographs.

Ray, Mary, and Andrea McHugh. *Dancing with Dogs*. San Diego, CA, Octopus Publishing Group Ltd., 2006. Freestyle moves and full routines explained with step-by-step photographs.

Reid, Pamela. *Excel-erated Learning: Explaining in Plain English How Dogs Learn and How Best to Teach Them*. Berkeley, CA, James & Kenneth Publishers, 1996. Learning theory in lay terms for quick and easy application.

Riddle, Maxwell. *Dogs Through History*. Fairfax, VA, Denlinger's Publishers, 1987. General work on the evolution of canines and the canine-human bond.

Ritvo, Harriet. *The Animal Estate: The English and Other Creatures in the Victorian Age*. Cambridge, MA, Harvard University Press, 1987. Interesting information about the beginning of the "pet age."

Rogers, Katharine. *First Friend: A History of Dogs and Humans*. New York, NY, St. Martin's Press, 2005. An in-depth exploration of the physical, emotional, and cultural ties between dogs and people throughout history.

Rogerson, John. *How to Get Your Dog to Play*. London, UK, Coronation Press Limited, 2004. Useful booklet with innovative ways to encourage your dog to play with you.

Rogerson, John. *The Dog Vinci Code*. London, UK, John Blake Publishing, Ltd., 2010. Engaging and unique approach to common behavioral and dog training problems.

Rugaas, Turid. *Barking: The Sound of a Language*. Wenatchee, WA, Dogwise Publications, 2008. Interesting perspective on dog-to-dog vocal communications.

Rugaas, Turid. *On Talking Terms with Dogs: Calming Signals*. Wenatchee, WA, Dogwise Publications, 2006. Fascinating, detailed examination of dog-to-dog non-vocal communications and how to use the same types of signals to communicate with your dog.

Schade, Victoria. *Bonding with Your Dog: A Trainer's Secrets for Building a Better Relationship*. Hoboken, NJ, Wiley Publishing, Inc., 2009. Exercises designed to help build a stronger relationship between you and your dog.

Scholz, Martina, and Clarissa von Reinhardt. *Stress in Dogs*. Wenatchee, WA, Dogwise Publishing, 2007. Useful primer for identifying the signs of canine stress and developing a plan to reduce stress.

Scott, John, and John Fuller. *Genetics and the Social Behavior of the Dog*. Chicago, IL, University of Chicago Press, 1965. Groundbreaking scientific study of the social development of dogs.

Serpell, James. *In the Company of Animals: A Study of Human-Animal Relationships*. Cambridge, UK, University Press, 1996. Exploration of the varied roles animals play in modern life.

Spector, Morgan. *Clicker Training for Obedience*. Waltham, MA, Sunshine Books, Inc., 1999. Comprehensive manual on clicker training for competitive obedience from Novice through Utility.

Stephanitz, Max von. *The German Shepherd Dog in Word and Picture*. Jena, Germany, Anton Kämpf, 1923. (In German). Definitive work by the father of the modern German Shepherd Dog.

Stephens, Henry. *The Book of the Farm*. Vol. II. Edinburgh and London, UK, William Blackwood and Sons, 1821. Contains information about early-nineteenth-century use of herding dogs in Great Britain.

Stifel, Robert. *The Dog Show: 125 Years of Westminster*. New York, NY, Westminster Kennel Club, 2001. Interesting insights into premier US dog show, with historical information on various early Westminster winners.

Stonehenge. *The Dog in Health and Disease*. London, UK, Longmans, Green, and Co., 1887. The seminal nineteenth-century reference to dogs commonly found in Great Britain.

Sundance, Kyra. *101 Dog Tricks*. Gloucester, MA, Quarry Books, 2007. Good basic trick-training book with excellent photographic explanations.

Theby, Viviane. *Dog University: A Training Program to Develop Advanced Skills with Your Dog*. Neptune City, NJ, T.F.H. Publications, Inc., 2009. Unique advanced trick training involving object identification, targeting, and task discrimination.

Tuan, Yi-Fu. *Dominance and Affection: The Making of Pets*. New Haven, CT, Yale University Press, 1984. Philosophical work on the reasons animals are kept as pets in modern society.

Yunck, Adele. *The Art of Proofing*. Ann Arbor, MI, Jabby Productions, 2008. Useful resource for improving reliability and generalizing competitive obedience behaviors that can also be adapted for use with everyday obedience behaviors.

Zeuner. F.E. *A History of Domesticated Animals*. London, UK, Hutchinson, 1963. Informative history of the human and domesticated-animal relationship.

## Videos and DVDs

Flanery, Julie. *T.A.P. Dancing for Success*. Boise, ID, Tawzer Dog LLC, 2011. Well-presented introduction to canine freestyle.

Kalnajs, Sarah. *The Language of Dogs: Understanding Canine Body Language and Other Communication Signals*. Wenatchee, WA, Dogwise Publishing, 2006. Video presentation of canine communication and behavior with accompanying commentary.

Nelson, Leslie. *Really Reliable Recall*. Manchester, CT, Healthy Dog Productions, 2004. Straightforward method for teaching your dog to come when called in an emergency.

Nijboer, Jan. *Treibball für Hunde*. Stuttgart, DE, Franckh–Kosmos Verlags–GmbH & Co. KG, 2007. (In German). Instructional DVD from the trainer who created the sport of Treibball (ball herding).

Pensinger, Sandi. *Beginning Treibball*. Boise, ID, Tawzer Dog LLC, 2011. Introduction to ball herding for all dog breeds.

Pensinger, Sandi. *Intermediate Treibball*. Boise, ID, Tawzer Dog LLC, 2011. Second in the series, explaining more advanced ball-herding skills.

## Selected Internet resources

American College of Veterinary Behaviorists. http://www.dacvb.org. Professional association for veterinary behaviorists. (3/3/15).

American Kennel Club. http://www.akc.org. Largest all-breed dog registry in the United States, also offering various competitive activities for herding dogs. (3/3/15).

Association of Professional Dog Trainers. http://apdt.com. Organization promoting humane training methods and trainer education. (3/3/15).

Certification Council for Professional Dog Trainers. http://ccpdt.org. Independent certification organization for dog trainers and behaviorists. (3/3/15).

Clothier, Suzanne. "He Just Wants to Say Hi!" http://suzanneclothier.com/the-articles/he-just-wants-say-hi. A must-read for all dog owners who take their dogs out in public. (3/3/15).

Dogfoodadvisor.com. http://m.vetmed.iastate.edu/vetapps/AdultBodyCondChart.pdf. Provides information and links to canine weight and nutrition topics, including the Purina Body Condition System chart. (3/3/15).

Fenzi, Denise. http://fenzidogsportsacademy.com/. Assorted online training courses with options for video feedback from qualified professional trainers. (3/3/15).

Gadbois, Simon. "It is not what you like, but what you want that counts: The neurochemistry of behaviour and motivation." https://www.facebook.com/photo.php?v=332329650267761&set=vb.124312344402827&type=2&theater. Presentation on current research in canine motivation at SPARCS Initiative 2014. (3/3/15).

Herdingontheweb.com. http://www.herdingontheweb.com. Comprehensive resource for herding dogs throughout the world. (3/3/15).

J & J Dog Supplies. http://www.jjdog.com. Well-established source of competitive obedience training supplies. (3/3/15).

Laurence, Kay. "Performance Jitters: Avoiding a Drop in Performance at Shows and Events." http://www.clickertraining.com/node/71. Explores benefits of delaying attachment of a performance cue until behavior is generalized. (3/3/15).

National Association of Dog Obedience Instructors. http://nadoi.org. One of the oldest professional organizations for obedience instructors. (3/3/15).

Nijboehr, Jan. http://www.natural-dogmanship.de. Website of the creator of treibball activity for herding dogs. (In German, Swiss, and English). (3/3/15).

Premier Dog Products. http://www.premier.com/store/. Great source for high-quality dog training products and toys. (3/3/15).

Rorem, Linda. "An Overview of Herding in France." http://www.herdingontheweb.com. Outstanding description of the various ways dogs are used throughout France. (3/3/15).

Rorem, Linda. "Tending the Flock." http://www.herdingontheweb.com. Historical review of various herding styles. (3/3/15).

United Kennel Club. http://www.ukcdogs.com/Web.nsf/WebPages/HRC/Home. Nationwide registry offering various competitive activities for herding dogs. (3/3/15).

Wwwmagyarvizslalu on Youtube.com. http://www.youtube.com/watch?v=ZSm5-e7uga4. (Are you fit enough for a Vizsla?) Thought-provoking video for anyone considering buying any high-energy dog. (3/3/15).

# About the Author

Since leaving the full-time practice of law in 2006 to become a professional dog trainer, Dawn Antoniak-Mitchell, Esq., MPA, CPDT-KSA, CBCC-KA, has helped dog owners and fellow dog trainers worldwide better understand and appreciate the role instincts play in family dog behavior and how to work with those instincts to help dogs achieve their full potential as enjoyable companions. She owns BonaFide Dog Academy LLC, an award-winning dog training facility in Omaha, NE.

Dawn has been a Certified Professional Dog Trainer–Knowledge and Skills Assessed (CPDT-KSA) since 2005, and is also a Certified Behavioral Consultant Canine–Knowledge Assessed (CBCC-KA), an American Kennel Club (AKC) obedience and rally obedience judge, an AKC Canine Good Citizen evaluator, and a World Cynosport rally obedience judge. A member of the Dog Writers Association of America, her work has appeared in local, regional, and national publications, including *Top Tips from Top Trainers*, published by the Association of Professional Dog Trainers. She has been interviewed nationally and internationally on a variety of dog-related topics. Dawn is the author of *Terrier-Centric Dog Training: From Tenacious to Tremendous* and *From Birdbrained to Brilliant: Teaching the Sporting Dog to Be a Great Companion*, both published by Dogwise Publications. Dawn is an advocate for the Americans with Disabilities Act (ADA) and service dogs. She has lectured at medical schools and disabled veterans' conferences about the ADA, the rights and responsibilities of service dog owners, and service dog training. She also worked as a behavioral consultant for a national dog food company.

Dawn has successfully competed with dogs from the herding, non-sporting, sporting, and terrier groups in a wide range of activities, including conformation, obedience, rally obedience, agility, tracking, scent work, earthdog tests, musical freestyle, and weight pulling. Several of her dogs have been nationally ranked in their respective sports. Her dogs regularly appear in local and national print and video productions and two of her dogs are therapy dogs who assist in school reading programs. Border Collie Gabriel is Dawn's current partner in a number of activities, including competitive obedience, rally obedience, tracking, musical freestyle, canicross, and caniteering.

*Dawn and her Border Collie, Gabriel.*

## Photo Credits

Dawn Antoniak-Mitchell and Border Collie Gabriel, Dalmatian Ember, and Jack Russell Terriers Lizzie B., Jinx, and Glitch; Jeff Bream and Curly-Coated Retriever Eli; Patty Mlsna Curry and Entlebucher Sennenhund Saphira; Gloria Hartshorn and Dutch Shepherd Zen (Robert Sanford, photographer); Kenny Hartshorn and Belgian Tervuren Cali (Robert Sanford, photographer); Dianne Krantz and Shetland Sheepdogs Dreamer, Lila, Princess, and Trooper; Cindy Mendonca and Bearded Collie Rorie; Melissa Myers and Miniature American Shepherd Treo; National Media Library under common use license; Ami Sheffield and Australian Shepherd Tazer; Carole Sewell and Cardigan Welsh Corgi Sully; Nate Standish and German Shepherd Dog Shishka; and Marabeth White and Dalmatians Carly and Panda.

# Index

Park it exercise, 109–114, 131–137
Pavlov, Ivan, 42
Pembroke Welsh Corgis, 11, 139
personal space, protection of, 2–3, 69–71, 116
physical exercise, 140–150
physical interaction, 61–62
play
    dog parks and, 38–40
    games to avoid, 101–102
    puppy classes and, 34–35
    as reward, 58–60
    socialization and, 32–33
predatory behavior, 19–23, 78, 101–102
Price, Carol, 27, 31, 104
punishment, 42–44
puppies, 30–38
Pyrenean Mastiffs, 13

## R
Red Heelers, 11
Reid, Pamela, 41
reinforcements
    delivery of, 64–67
    overview, 42–44
    types of, 54–63
release cue, 77–78, 97–99
Respect the Bubble management technique, 2–3, 69–71, 116
rewards
    delivery of, 64–67
    overview, 42–44
    types of, 54–63
Riddle, Maxwell, 6
Rogerson, John, 30
Rorem, Linda, 8, 27
Rottweilers, 14

## S
sheepdogs, 7, 14
Shetland Sheepdogs, 14, 31, 101, 125
socialization
    classes and, 34–38
    dog parks and doggie daycare, 38–40
    overview, 30–33
Speak with quiet exercise, 128–131
spinning, 26, 119–124
stages of learning, 45–46
stay exercises, 109–119
Stay means stay exercise, 115–119
stop and drop exercise, 78–86
Stop the spin cycle exercise, 119–124

stress
    coping techniques, 75
    effects on behavior, 51

## T
tenacity of herding dogs
    defined, 26–27
    management techniques, 101–103
    training exercises, 103–124
*Tending the Flock* (Rorem), 8
*Terrier-Centric Dog Training: From Tenacious to Tremendous* (Antoniak-Mitchell), 2
terriers, 16, 18, 21–22
toys, 58–60, 63
training. *See also* exercises
    for barking issues, 128–137
    compared to management, 52–53
    for control issues and frustration threshold, 77–99
    for exceptional energy and über-intelligence, 150–152
    for tenacity, focus, and obsessiveness, 103–124
treats, 56–58, 94–95. *See also* reinforcements
trick training, 144–150
triggers, identification of, 115–116
Tuan, Yi-Fu, 41

## U
Über-intelligence of herding dogs
    management techniques, 138–150
    overview, 28–29
    training exercises, 150–152

## V
verbal interaction, 61–62, 123–124, 126
von Stephanitz, Capt. Max, 8–9, 25

## W
walking behavior
    barking issues, 128–131
    exercises for, 86–94, 120–123
    protection of personal space, 2–3, 69–71, 116
Walking in a straight line exercise, 86–94
Welsh Corgis, 11–12
windows behavior, 126–127
working/obedience intelligence, 28

## Y
You talkin' to me? exercise, 95–97

# Also available from Dogwise Publishing

Go to www.dogwise.com for more books and ebooks.

## From Birdbrained to Brilliant
### Training the Sporting Dog to be a Great Companion
Dawn Antoniak-Mitchell

Sporting dog breeds can be relatively easy to train to do what they have been bred to do be it retrieve, point, flush—even act as a decoy to attract game! In this book, author Dawn Antoniak-Mitchell offers answers to solving and preventing the often surprising set of problems that owners of sporting dogs encounter at home and in their local communities.

## Terrier-Centric Dog Training
### From Tenacious to Tremendous
Dawn Antoniak-Mitchell

In *Terrier-Centric Dog Training*, author Dawn Antoniak-Mitchell takes up the challenge to help terrier owners train their dogs by making sure they understand the instincts bred into terriers and what the most effective training and management techniques are to use when working with a "natural born killer." You can train your terrier, but just don't let him loose off-leash in a park full of squirrels!

## Canine Body Language
### A Photographic Guide
Brenda Aloff

Canine Body Language by Brenda Aloff is a guide to canine body language. Never before has the body language of dogs been so thoroughly documented with photographs and text. Hundreds of images in this almost 400 page book illustrate the incredible variety of postures, behaviors and situations that the typical dog either manifests or encounters in his day-to-day life.

*Winner of the 2006 DWAA Maxwell Award: Best General Reference Book*

## On Talking Terms with Dogs, 2nd Ed.
### Calming Signals
Turid Rugaas

Norwegian dog trainer and behaviorist Turid Rugaas is a noted expert on canine body language, notably "calming signals," which are signals dogs use to avoid conflict, invite play, and communicate a wide range of information to other dogs and people. These are the dogs' attempt to defuse situations that otherwise might result in fights or aggression. Companion DVD, *Calming Signals: What Your Dog Tells You*, is also available. The DVD shows footage of many calming signals, how dogs use them, and how you can use them to calm your dog.

Dogwise.com is your source for quality books, ebooks, DVDs, training tools and treats.

We've been selling to the dog fancier for more than 25 years and we carefully screen our products for quality information, safety, durability and FUN! You'll find something for every level of dog enthusiast on our website www.dogwise.com or drop by our store in Wenatchee, Washington.

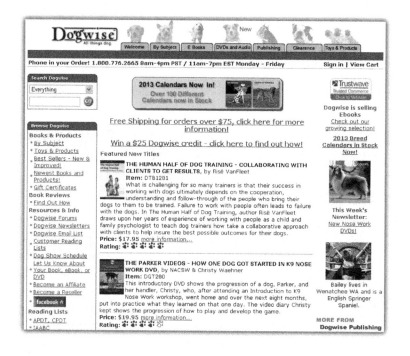